CYCLING
around
STAFFORDSHIRE

Compiled by Arnold Robinson

THE JOHN MERRILL FOUNDATION
2008

Cycling around Series

ISBN 1-874754-57-8

1

THE JOHN MERRILL FOUNDATION,
32, Holmesdale,
Waltham Cross,
Hertfordshire
EN8 8QY
Tel/Fax 01992 - 762776
email - marathonhiker@aol.com

Printed, bound, marketed and distributed by The John Merrill Foundation.

© Text, - Arnold Robinson 1999
© Additional text - John N. Merrill 1999
© Maps - Arnold Robinson 1999.

First Published - November 1999
This reprint - January 2008.

ISBN 1 874754 57 8

British Library Cataloguing-in-Publication Data.
A catalogue record for this book is available from the British Library.

Please note - The maps in this guide are purely illustrative. You are encouraged to use the appropriate 1:50,000 O.S. map.

Meticulous research has been undertaken to ensure that this publication is highly accurate at the time of going to press. The publishers, however, cannot be held responsible for alterations, errors or omissions, but they would welcome notification of such for future editions.

Typeset in AGaramond - bold, italic and plain 10pt, 14pt and 18pt.

Printed by - The John Merrill Foundation
Designed and typset by The John Merrill Foundation

Cover photograph - by Arnold Robinson

Cover design© The John Merrill Foundation

Arnold Robinson rides through the ford at Wetton Mill
midway along the Manifold Way - Ride No.3.

ABOUT THE AUTHOR

Arnold Robinson was born in Staffordshire - at Burton-Upon-Trent - and he lived in the county for the first few years of his life. He commenced school at Uttoxeter.

He has been a dedicated cyclist for sixty years. In that time, he has cycled in every county in England and Wales, each region of Scotland, in Ireland and Europe. He first cycled in Lincolnshire in the thirties and has returned on many occasions to explore the cycling byways, its towns and especially its villages.

After spending most of his childhood in Derbyshire and Nottinghamshire, in 1939 he moved to Sheffield to join the Police Force. When he retired in 1969, he held the rank of Detective Chief Superintendent and was head of the Criminal Investigation Department of Sheffield and Rotherham. After a spell as Police Consultant to Yorkshire Television and in industrial security, he became a freelance writer, broadcaster and photographer on outdoor activities but mainly cycling.

He regularly contributes articles and photographs to cycling magazines and is the author of a series of regional cycling guides covering the whole of Britain. He was also a major contributor of routes for *'Cyclists' Britain'* published in 1985 by Ordnance Survey/Pan Books.

His first of nearly two hundred broadcasts on cycling was made In 1939. This was an outside broadcast from the Priest's House at Kings Mill at Castle Donnington. For five years he was the presenter of BBC Radio Sheffield's cycling programme *'On your Bike'*.

3

CYCLING ROUTES AROUND STAFFORDSHIRE

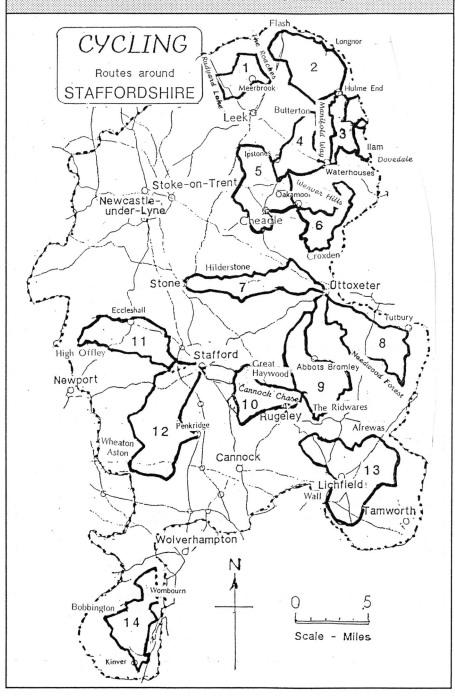

CYCLING

Routes around

STAFFORDSHIRE

4

CONTENTS

Key to ROUTE MAPS;

Cycling Routes.

Alternative Cycling Routes.

Main Roads.

Other Roads.

Unsurfaced roads and tracks.

Railways.

Rivers/Streams.

Lakes/Reservoirs.

Built up areas.

Towns/Villages.

Church.

Youth Hostel.

Camp Site.

Places of interest.

Summit.

Viewpoint.

KEY TO ABBREVIATIONS in ITINERARIES:

Inf: Tourist Information Office.
EC   Early Closing Day.
MD   Market Day.
BR: British Railway Passenger Station.
B&B   Bed & Breakfast accomodation.
YH   Youth Hostel.
Cafe   Cafe or Restaurant.
PM   Pub Meals.
Sh   Shops supplying food.
T: Toilets.
Cmg: Camp Sites.
Cvg: Caravan sites.
Sp: Signpost.
TR: Traffic island.
TL: Traffic lights.

An Introduction to Cycling around Staffordshire.

Staffordshire offers a wide choice of cycling routes through a very varied terrain ranging from the hills and wild moorland of the Peak District in the north to the softer and mellow countryside of the heart of the county passing on the way the dramatic views from Cannock Chase and crossing the Trent Valley. Much of the centre of the county is devoted to dairy farming.

The River Trent rises to the west of Stoke-on-Trent but does not become of interest to a tourist until it has passed through Trentham Gardens from where it turns south east to Rugeley. At Alrewas, the river turns north and for a few miles forms the county boundary with Derbyshire. On the west the River Dove forms the county boundary with Derbyshire and in this region is some of the best of the scenery.

Although Staffordshire is crossed by the M6 and M54 motorways and many other busy trunk roads, there is still an extensive network of country byroads ideal for relaxed cycling. Beginners and family groups will find the routes described in this guide ideal as it is along these byways that the best of the scenery will be found.

The only industrial and heavily built up areas of the county are around the Potteries - Stoke-on-Trent and Newcastle-under-Lyme: a small area around Cannock and in the south, the border with the West Midlands. When planning cycling routes in Stafford-shire it is therefore advisable to avoid these areas. Some of the main roads in and around Stafford, Lichfield and Cannock, each of which has modern industrial estates, may also occasionally be congested but the smaller towns -Leek, Cheadle, Stone, Uttoxeter and Rugeley are relatively quiet and present no serious problems to cyclists who can quickly reach the open country.

My first cycling in Staffordshire was in May 1935 when I discovered the Manifold Valley, still one of my favourite corners of the county. I returned again in 1937 to visit the Youth Hostel at Rudyard Lake (long since closed). Since then I have made regular visits and have cycled all the routes described in this guide some of them on many occasions.

I have selected my favourite rides which present the county's different faces, the many places of interest, its most attractive villages and byways.

THE ROUTES.

The routes have been designed, so far as is practicable, to follow quiet byways so avoiding the heavy traffic which bedevils the main roads on summer weekends and during the holiday periods. By keeping to the byways, it is possible to ride for long periods seeing few motor vehicles.

Each of the rides could form the basis for a 'day ride' or be combined into an on going tour. The rides could be commenced or finished at any point around the circuit, eg. Ride No.7 could be started at either Uttoxeter as indicated or at Stone.

Some of the rides have optional extensions (see Notes at foot of the itineraries). The mileage might be reduced by using one or more of the alternative routes indicated on the maps. The only really strenuous rides are those in the north of the county where this borders on to the Peak District and to a lesser degree. Ride No.10 around Cannock Chase. Experienced riders might be able to cover two of the rides in one day.

Cyclists who are adept at planning their own routes will find the 'Touring information' useful when looking for a 'new route' or a variation of past tours.

PLACES OF INTEREST.
On all the suggested rides, there are places of historical, scenic and/or general interest. In particular visits to the following are recommended.

Ride No.1. Rudyard Trail and Narrow Gauge Railway. Tittesworth Country Park, The Roaches, Hen Cloud and Ramshaw Rocks.
Ride No.2. Longnor Market Hall, Hollins Hill, Chrome Hill, Washgate Packhorse Bridge, Flash, Three Shires Head.
Ride No.3. The Manifold Way (one of the finest 'off-highway' cycling routes in the country), Thor's Cave, Beeston Tor, Throwley Hall: Ilam Hall, Dovedale and the Stepping Stones, Milldale, Alstonfield, Beresford Dale.
Ride No. 4. Back O' the Brook, Froghall Canal Wharf.
Ride No. 5. Froghall Canal Wharf, Cheddleton Railway Centre, Consall Nature Park, Foxfield Railway Centre, Hawksmoor Nature Reserve.
Ride No.6. Churnet Valley (a beautiful cycling route), Alton, Croxden Abbey, Ellastone (associated with story of 'Adam Bede'), Weaver Hills, view point.
Ride No.8. Tutbury - Castle and church; Needwood Forest.
Ride No.9. Abbots Bromley - horn dance, Hoar Cross - church; Ridware villages;
Ride No.10 Cannock Chase Country Park, Military Cemetery, Forest Visitors Centre, Great Haywood - Essex Bridge and Shugborough Hall and Park, Tixall Gatehouse.
Ride No.11. High Offley - Shropshire Union Canal, Eccleshall - castle ruins: Shallowford - Isaac Walton's cottage.
Ride No.12. Breewood (pronounced Brood) - Speedwell Castle, Chillington Hall, Boscobel Oak, Greenway Cycle Trail.
Ride No.13. Lichfield Cathedral, Fradley Canal Junction, Wall - Roman Station.
Ride No.14. Wombourn - Kingswinford Trail, Kinver - rocks and view point.

THE TOWNS.
Some of the smaller towns - Leek, Cheadle, Uttoxeter, Rugeley, Lichfield and even Stafford - are worth exploring when cycling in the vicinity.

THE VILLAGES.
There is little doubt that it is STAFFORDSHIRE's villages which cyclists will find the most attractive, eg.

Ride No.1. Meerbrook, Rudyard, Upper Hulme.
Ride No.2. Longnor, Flash, Upper Elkstone, Warslow.
Ride No.3. Ilam, Milldale, Alstonfield.
Ride No.4. Waterfall, Grindon, Ipstones, Froghall.
Ride No.5. Oakamoor, Froghall, Consall.
Ride No.6. Alton, Croxden, Ellastone, Wootton, Farley.
Ride No.7. Milwich, Cotwalton, Hilderstone, Church Leigh.
Ride No.8. Marchington, Tutbury, Tattenhall, Dunstall, Newborough.
Ride No.9. Abbots Bromley, Hamstall Ridware, Mavesyn Ridware.
Ride No.10. Milford, Brockton, Little Haywood, Great Haywood, Tixall.
Ride No.11. Most of the villages around the circuit.
Ride No.12. Levedale, Breewood, Wheaton Aston.
Ride No.13. Longdon Green, Alrewas, Harlaston, Elford, Weeford.
Ride No.14. Greensforge, Kinver, Enville, Halfpenny Green, Trysull.

ACCOMMODATION.
There are three Youth Hostels in Staffordshire, all in the north east corner, (see page 66-68), and Gradbach just over the border in Cheshire.

There are facilities for other accommodation including overnight 'Bed and Breakfast'. Details from the Information Offices at Stafford and Leek.

WHERE TO EAT.
On most of the routes there is a choice of places to eat ranging from restaurants and pub meals to tea rooms. The location of these are shown in the itineraries but on routes which pass through the more remote areas, it is advisable to carry emergency supplies of food and drink.

CYCLE HIRE and REPAIRS.
There are Cycle Hire facilities at Waterhouses at the southern end of the Manifold Valley and at Rudyard Lake.

There are cycle shops at Burton-on-Trent, Lichfield, Newcastle-under-Lyme, Leek, Stoke-on-Trent and Tamworth and, in an emergency, the Cycle Hire Centres may be able to assist.

MAPS.
The route maps are sufficiently detailed within the scope of the scale to enable the itinerary to be followed without difficulty but greater detail will be found on Ordnance Survey Landranger maps. Sheets Nos. 118, 1190, 127, 128, 138 and 139 cover the routes.

RIDE NO.1
RUDYARD LAKE, TITTESWORTH RESERVOIR
AND THE ROACHES - 17.5 MILES

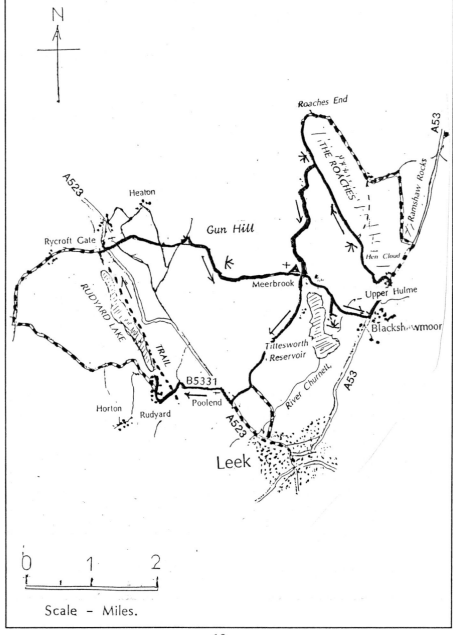

Scale - Miles.

RIDE NO. 1
RUDYARD LAKE, TITTESWORTH RESERVOIR and THE ROACHES
- 17.5 MILES

Start: Meerbrook (Youth Hostel).
Car Park, Tittesworth Country Park off A53 Buxton - Leek road.

The route for this ride is divided into two loops both of which are strenuous. The first loop of 10.5 miles is to RUDYARD LAKE then continue along the Rudyard Lake Trail. The second half of the ride climbs up to the Roaches with an optional extension to make a circuit of one of the most prominent heights in the county.

GRADIENTS: The first 6.5 miles which includes the RUDYARD TRAIL is relatively easy but there is then a long and often steep climb to Gun Hill. This is followed by an easy descent back to Meerbrook. The second loop includes a steep climb from Upper Hulme continuing along the side of the ROACHES.

Miles.	Places and route itinerary.	Information and Points of Interest.
	MEERBROOK. Turn L (opp YH) and climb steadily above Reservoir; in half-mile descend and in 1m after another short climb, turn R (opp stone gate); desc. to T junc (A523) and turn R into:	YH. PM. T. Church: 1870. Small village adjoining the Tittesworth Reservoir. At the time of its construction, the village was threatened with being submerged but it was finally spared.
2.5	**POOLEND.** Turn L on B5231 (sp Rudyard); in 1m pass under bridge and climb to TR; then R into:	Hamlet on Leek-Macclesfield road. Sh. Delightful village. Memorial to Boer War. Rudyard Kipling was named after Rudyard as his parents spent their honeymoon here. Popular resort in Victoria times. The reservoir was constructed to feed the Trent and Mersey Canal but is now primarily used for water sports.
1.5	**RUDYARD.** Imm. fork R to RUDYARD LAKE; (optional diversion to Lakeside) retrace route to TR and turn L; in half-mile turn R into yard of former railway station; turn sharp L on	
0.5	**RUDYARD TRAIL.** Follow TRAIL alongside Reservoir to its exit; turn R on byroad, cross bridge and climb to X rds (A523) at:	Surface is loose gravel but it is level and easy riding. Narrow gauge railway runs for one mile alongside the Trail.

Miles.	Places and route itinerary.	Information and Points of Interest.
2.5	**RYCROFT GATE,** Cont str ahead on narrow byroad; climb steeply; at X rds continue ahead climbing steeply at times to X rds; cont ahead and then turn R (sp Meerbrook); climb for further 1m to summit of Gun Hill then descend to:	Junction on Leek-Macclesfield road. Care when crossing as visibility is restricted. Views to west across Cheshire Plain.
3.5	**MEERBROOK.** Continue through village and in half-mile turn R through gate into:	See above.
0.5	**TITTESWORTH WATER.** Return to gate and turn R; climb to T junc (A53) at:	Popular Country Park. T. Bird Hide. Visitors Centre. Cafe - limited opening in winter.
1	**BLACKSHAWMOOR.** Turn L and in 1m after bridge (River Churnet), turn L (sp Upper Hulme); continue into:	Busy main road.
1	**UPPER HULME.** Turn L across bridge and continue past works then climb very steeply for half-mile; continue to climb passing close to HEN CLOUD and alongside THE ROACHES; in 2m turn L (sp Meerbrook) (See note a) and descend steeply at first to:	Small village below Hen Cloud. It was originally on the main road but is now bypassed. Roaches Tea Rooms on L. Impressive rock formations. Views of Tittesworth Reservoir.
4.5	**MEERBROOK.**	

NOTES:
(a) Alternative route after RUDYARD: at Memorial, fork L up hill; climb then descend steeply followed by another steep climb to X rds; descend steeply then climb to T junc; turn R on byroad. At bridge join main route where it leaves the RUDYARD TRAIL.
(b). Alternative route making circuit of THE ROACHES and the RAMSHAW ROCKS. Continue straight ahead on gated road to ROACHES END; after passing through second gate, turn R along east side of THE ROACHES; in 2m turn sharp R on narrow byroad alongside RAMSHAW ROCKS; descend to T junc (A53); turn R then descend to BLACKSHAW MOOR and retrace outward route to MEERBROOK. (See map).

A picturesque corner in the hamlet of Upper Hulme below The Roaches Ride No.1.

The spires of Lichfield Cathedral rise above the houses of the town (Ride No.13).

RIDE NO. 2
LONGNOR, HOLLINSCLOUGH,
FLASH and WARSLOW - 21.5 MILES

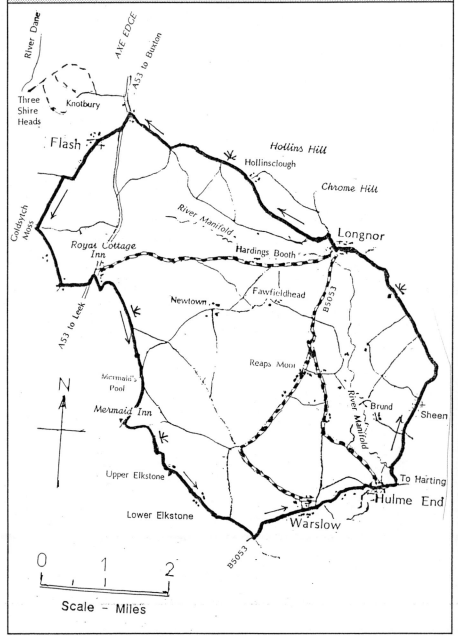

14

RIDE NO. 2
LONGNOR,
HOLLINSCLOUGH,
FLASH and WARSLOW
- 21.5 MILES

Start: Hulme End, on B5054 2m W. Hartington.

Car Park: Old Railway Station, Hulme End.

This ride starts along the northern boundary of Staffordshire with Derbyshire. As it climbs into the Peak District hills with the valleys of the River Dove on one side and the Manifold on the other, there are some fantastic views of wild terrain. There are several quaint corners at Longnor and along the route are two notable Inns, the 'Travellers Rest' at Flash and the 'Mermaid' at the northern end of the Morridge. From the 'Travellers Rest' there is an optional extension of the ride to Three Shire Heads (see note d).

GRADIENTS: The first ten miles involve almost continuous climbing including several very steep hills with corresponding steep descents on which care is required. There are some long easy descents on the return.

Miles.	Places and route itinerary.	Information and Points of Interest.
	HULME END: At Car Park Exit, turn R; continue through village, cross bridge and after short climb, turn L on byroad (sp Sheen); climb to X rds and cont str ahead through:	Sh. B&B. Cvg. Cmg. Car Park was northern terminus of former Manifold Valley Light Railway; now a popular cycling TRAIL. (see note a).
2	**SHEEN.** Continue ahead along ridge road then desc, steeply at times to:	PM. B&B. Quiet farming village on ridge between Dove and Manifold valleys. Church: 1852, Cross. Extensive views of Peak District hills.
2	**LONGNOR.** At X rds in centre of village, turn R and in half-mile turn L (sp Hollinsclough); after short desc turn R through valley to:	PM. Sh. T. C. Unspoiled small town with several quaint corners. Market Hall, notice of tolls. Church: 1780. Wakes Festival, 1st week in Sept. (see note b).

Miles	Places and route itinerary.	Information and Points of Interest.
2	**HOLLINSCLOUGH.** Cont ahead and climb very steeply for half-mile; cont ahead at sign ' Unfit for Motors', then desc steeply on very narrow byroad; again climb steeply and cont to T junc; turn R and continue to:	Church 19 cent. Remote village in fold of hills in Upper Dove Valley. Views of Chrome Hill and Parkhouse Hill to R. At foot of desc, green track on R leads to WASHGATE picturesque packhorse bridge. Diversion recommended. Half-mile return.
2.5	**TRAVELLER'S REST INN.** Turn L on A53 and in half-mile, turn R to:	Sh. a well known landmark at road junc on Buxton-Leek road at southern most point of Axe Edge; road is frequently closed by winter snow. The highest point of the ride, 1518 ft. altitude. (see note a).
1	**FLASH.** Fork L at church and desc for 1m; imm after RH bend, turn L (sp Goldsytch) into byroad; climb and continue to road junction at:	PM. Church: 1901 One of the highest villages in England altitude 1518 ft. From here, rivers run west to Irish Sea and east to North Sea.
2	**GOLDSYTCH MOSS.** At road junc fork L (sp Royal Cottage Inn); climb steadily and towards summit, bear L and continue to X rds (A53) near:	A bleak open area to north of Roaches.
1	**ROYAL COTTAGE INN.** Cont str ahead through wild country. Bear R at road junction and in 2m desc to:	Inn in remote location on A53 Buxton-Leek road. Wild open countryside. Extensive views: Ramshaw Rocks, Hen Cloud, Tittesworth Reservoir.
2.5	**MERMAID INN.** Turn L opp Inn and in half-mile turn R on byroad; in half-mile fork L and then descend steeply through:	Mermaid Pool on R.
1.5	**UPPER ELKSTONE.** Cont to desc, steeply at times:	Cmg. B&B. Small farming village.
1	**LOWER ELKSTONE.** Cont ahead to T junc (B5053); turn L to:	The start of pastoral countryside.

Miles.	Places and route itinerary.	Information and Points of Interest.
2	WARSLOW. Cont ahead and in half-mile turn R on byroad (sp Ecton); fork L on grass grown lane and desc steeply to T junc (B5054) turn R to:	PM. T. B&B. Camping Barn. Centre of small village to L.
2	HULME END.	

NOTES:
(a)   From HULME END , there is an alternative and slightly shorter route to LONGNOR: turn L in village and follow byroads west side of River Dove (see map).
(b) From LONGNOR, there are several shorter alternative routes via either Reaps Moor or Hardings Booth (see map).
(c) 11/2 miles W of the Traveller's Rest in the Dane Valley, is a picturesque packhorse bridge at Three Shire Heads. Here the counties of Staffordshire, Derbyshire and Cheshire meet. The bridge can only be reached by unsurfaced rough tracks. (See map).

The River Manifold is frequently 'dry' at Weag's Bridge. The flow of water eventually reappears in the grounds of Ilam Hall (Ride No.3).

17

RIDE NO. 3
MANIFOLD WAY, WATERHOUSES, ILAM
DOVEDALE & ALSTONFIELD - 32 MILES

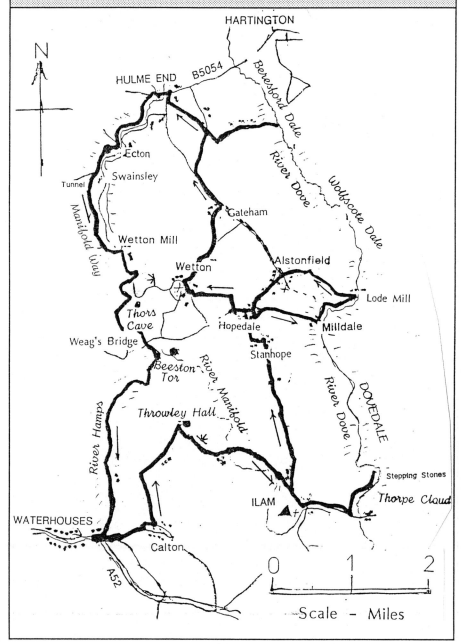

RIDE NO. 3
MANIFOLD WAY, WATERHOUSES, ILAM, DOVEDALE & ALSTONFIELD
-32 MILES

Start: Hulme End, on B50454 2m W of Hartington.

Car Park: Old Railway Station, Hulme End.

The first eight miles are along the Manifold Way, a popular off highway cycling route. From Waterhouses, the route then crosses the hills to Ilam from where there is an optional extension to Dovedale which the county shares with Derbyshire. The return route links some picturesque villages - Milldale, Alstonfield and Wetton and there is a final optional diversion to Beresford Dale which has associations with Isaac Walton, of angling fame.

GRADIENTS: After the first easy eight miles along the Manifold Way, this ride is a succession of climbs many of them strenuous. There is a steep climb from Waterhouses to Calton and a long descent past Throwley Hall into the Manifold valley. There is then another climb and a steep descent into Ilam. On leaving Ilam, there is another climb but the gradients ease as Stanhope is approached. The diversion to Milldale and Lode Mill starts with a descent and there is then another steep climb to Alstonfield. This is followed by a descent to Hopedale and another climb to Wetton after which the gradients are undulating.

Miles.	Places and route itinerary.	Information and Points of Interest.
	HULME END. From Car Park turn along MANI-FOLD WAY and continue to crossing at:	Sh. B&B. Cvg. Cmg. Car Park is on site of northern terminus of MANI-FOLD VALLEY LIGHT RAILWAY Closed in 1934. TRAIL is surfaced and one of the finest off highway cycling routes in the country.
1	ECTON. Continue on Trail to:	Site of former Copper Mine. A by-road on the right descends from WARSLOW. Around here the TRAIL runs alongside the River Manifold (see note a).
1	SWAINSLEY. Continue ahead through tunnel and continue on TRAIL to:	Tunnel is illuminated by overhead lights. (See note b). This section of the TRAIL is also used by light vehicles, care required.

Miles	Places and route itinerary.	Information and Points of Interest.
1	**WETTON MILL.** Continue on TRAIL (or fork R through ford and continue on byroad) to:	Cafe, drinks and snacks. Cmg. T. Caves. Ford in picturesque location. In dry weather, river flows underground finally reappearing at ILAM (see later).
1	**REDHURST CROSSING:** Continue on TRAIL to:	Byroad to L climbs very steeply to WETTON. Thor's Cave in hillside on L.
1	**WEAG'S BRIDGE.** Continue ahead on TRAIL to:	Byroad on R climbs very steeply to GRINDON (see Ride No.4). Beeston Tor (NT) on L. TRAIL now continues through HAMPS Valley. In 2m Tea Room/Gardens on L.
3	**WATERHOUSES.** At end of TRAIL turn L on A523 climb for half mile then fork L; climb steeply to outskirts of:	PM. Sh. Cycle Hire. Care required when leaving TRAIL as traffic on A523 is usually heavy.
1	**CALTON.** Fork L and in half mile, turn L on narrow byroad; climb for 1m then desc (gated road) to:	Quiet village in secluded location off A523. Extensive views. Wild open country.
2	**THROWLEY HALL.** Pass through farmyard and then desc through open fields; in 1.5 miles at farm entrance, turn L; cross bridge (River Manifold) and climb then continue to T Junc; turn R and desc steeply into:	Farm. Ruins of Hall.\n\nView of Manifold Valley on L.
2.5	**ILAM.** Fork L and in half-mile turn L on narrow byroad (NOT Hotel entrance) to:	B&B. YH. Hall (NT) C. Saxon Church. Cross. Unspoiled village with attractive cottages. River Manifold reappears after flowing underground.
1.5	**DOVEDALE.** Continue to Stepping Stones and then retrace route to:	Popular location often crowded and best avoided at holiday times. Stepping Stones cross river to Derbyshire side.

Miles.	Places and route itinerary.	Information and Points of Interest.
1.5	**ILAM.** Fork R and climb very steeply for 1m then continue to:	See above.
3.5	**STANHOPE.** Continue ahead and desc to T junc; turn R (see note c) and desc to T junc at:	B&B. Farming hamlet.
2	**HOPEDALE.** Turn R past Inn and desc on narrow byroad through valley to:	PM. Hamlet in secluded valley.
1	**MILLDALE.** Continue alongside river to:	Snacks. T. Delightful spot on River Dove which here forms county boundary with Derbyshire. Viator's Bridge.
1	**LODE MILL.** Turn sharp L and climb steeply for 1m to:	Lovely spot where bridge crosses River Dove at foot of Wolfescote Dale. Snowdrops on banks in spring.
1	**ALSTONFIELD.** Turn L at green (see note d) and desc to junc at:	B&B. PM. C. T. Church; 15 cent with Norman doorway and chancel, Saxon Crosses. Box pews. Charles Cotton pew. Lane past Church descends steeply to MILLDALE (see MILLDALE). Artists studio.
1	**HOPEDALE.** Turn R and climb steeply; in half-mile turn R and continue to:	See above.
1.5	**WETTON.** Turn R into village and again turn R opp. Inn; continue on narrow byroad to road junc at:	PM. B&B. T. Cvg. Cmg. Church: 1820 with 16 cent tower. Peaceful village above Manifold Valley.
1.5	**GATEHAM.** At X rds turn L and in half-mile turn R (see note d); desc to X rds and turn R (sp Beresford Dale); desc to footbridge at end of:	Farm. Cvg. Cmg.
2	**BERESFORD DALE.** Retrace route to X rds and continue str ahead; desc to T junc and turn R; desc to T Junc (B5054) and turn L across bridge into:	Lovely location. Made famous by Isaac Walton. Walk through Dale to Pike Pool recommended. Fishing Lodge. Footbridge across river gives access to byroad to HARTINGTON (see map)
2	**HULME END.**	

NOTES:
(a)   There is an alternative route via a byroad along the east side of the Valley which leads direct to ECTON (See map).
(b)   To avoid the tunnel, turn L, cross bridge and then turn R through gate on byroad which is narrow and badly surfaced.
(c) The mileage may be reduced by four miles by omitting the diversion to MILLDALE, LODE MILL AND ALSTONFIELD: Turn L and ride direct to WETTON then continue as main route.
(d)   The diversion to BERESFORD DALE may be omitted and the distance reduced by four miles, by riding direct to HULME END.

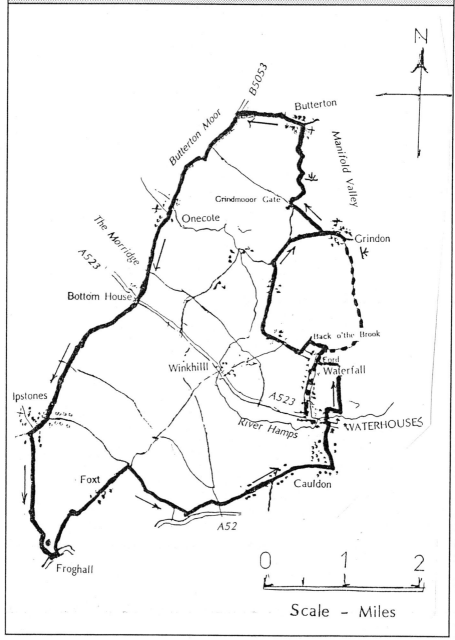

RIDE NO. 4
BUTTERTON, ONECOTE,
IPSTONES, and FROGHALL

- 22.5 MILES

Start: Waterhouses on A52 Leek-Ashbourne road.
Car Park: Waterhouses, Old Railway Station. (Cycle Hire Centre).

This is a very varied ride through the Staffordshire Moorlands District in the south west corner of the Peak District National Park. It includes many attractive corners and some little visited villages away from main roads and the usual tourist routes. eg Grindon, Butterton, Ipstones and Foxt. Much of the terrain is wild. From the exposed high ground, there are extensive views, the only dull spot being around the cement works at Cauldon.

GRADIENTS: The ride starts with a climb to GRINDON and then a steep descent and a further climb to BUTTERTON. There is a climb on leaving ONECOTE and a very steep descent from IPSTONES to FROGHALL. This is followed by a steep climb through FOXT. Care is required on the steep descent to the ford at BUTTERTON and on the last mile from IPSTONES TO FROGHALL.

Miles.	Places and route itinerary.	Information and Points of Interest.
	WATERHOUSES. At Car Park Exit, turn R to junc A523; cross over into narrow by-road; cross bridge and turn R; climb very steeply on narrow byroad and continue to:	PM. Sh. Cyc Hire. Road has poor surface.
1	**WATERFALL.** Fork R and desc to:	Church: screen, panelling. Peaceful village, water pump, stocks
0.5	**BACK O' THE BROOK.** Pass through ford and imm turn L; (see note a); climb to T junc; turn R and continue climbing keeping to R at all junctions; desc into:	Quiet hamlet, ford is usually shallow.
3	**GRINDON.** Retrace route for half-mile and fork R; climb to:	PM. B&B. Moorland village. Church: 1884 has Norman font and prominent spire. Memorial to RAF crew killed when their plane crashed when flying in food when village was cut off by snow. Views of Manifold valley.

23

Miles	Places and route itinerary.	Information and Points of Interest.
1	**GRINDMOOR GATE.** Turn R at Tel. Kiosk on winding by-road; in 1m desc very steeply to Ford (raised pavement available when stream flooded); climb very steeply into:	Bleak junction of byroads.
1.5	**BUTTERTON.** Turn L and continue through village on byroad; continue to T junc (B5053); turn L across BUTTERTON MOOR then descend through:	B&B. Cafe near ford. Sh. Church, 1871, spire. Moorland village of stone cottages.
3	**ONECOTE.** Continue ahead and climb for 1.5m to X rds; cont straight ahead and desc to:	Straggling village at junction of B5053 and byroad to Leek. Church: 1755.
1.5	**BOTTOM HOUSE.** At X rds continue straight ahead and climb to X rds; continue straight ahead and descend through:	Hamlet on Leek-Ashbourne road. Wild open countryside with extensive views.
2.5	**IPSTONES.** Continue ahead and descend steeply to:	Large village on high ground above Churnet valley. Interesting old houses. 1m, W is Belmont House. Chapel House. Devil's Staircase which descends into Churnet valley.
2	**FROGHALL.** At junc with A52, turn L and in 200 yds turn L on byroad passing:	Small village in Churnet valley.
0.5	**FROGHALL WHARF.** Climb for 1.5 miles, very steeply at times, to:	Picturesque spot on Caldon Canal. Site of former copper and brass foundry. Narrow boat trips.
1.5	**FOXT.** Continue ahead and in half-mile at X rds turn R; in 1m (imm prior to junc with A52); turn L on byroad; in half-mile at X rds continue str ahead; at T junc turn L then desc through:	Small village on edge of moorlands Newfield Gallery, open to public.

24

Miles.	Places and route itinerary.	Information and Points of Interest.
3.5	CAULDON. Continue ahead and desc to:	Church: 18 cent. Moorland village spoiled by close proximity to cement works.
1	WATERHOUSES.	

NOTES:

(a) From BACK o'the BROOK, there is an alternative route to GRINDON. Imm after the ford, turn R and climb on narrow byroad and then continue on track. The surface is very rough in middle section.

(b) From WATERHOUSES, there is an alternative and more direct route to WATER-FALL. (See map).

FROGHALL WHARF is a picturesque spot on the Caldon Canal.

25

RIDE NO.5
AROUND CHEADLE
- FROGHALL and CHEDDLETON - 27 MILES

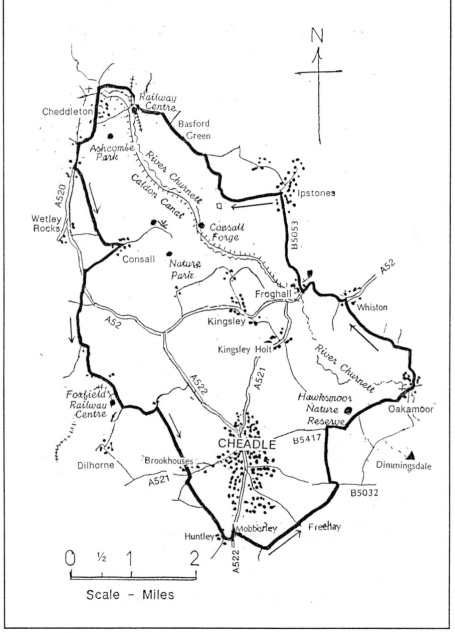

N

Cheddleton

Railway Centre

Basford Green

Ashcombe Park

River Churnett

Caldon Canal

A520

Wetley Rocks

Consall

Nature Park

Consall Forge

Ipstones

B5053

A52

Froghall

Whiston

Kingsley

A52

Kingsley Holt

River Churnett

A522

A521

Foxfield Railway Centre

Hawksmoor Nature Reserve

Oakamoor

CHEADLE

B5417

Dimmingsdale

Dilhorne

Brookhouses

A521

Huntley

Mobberley

Freehay

A522

B5032

0   ½   1   2

Scale - Miles

RIDE NO. 5
AROUND CHEADLE.
Froghall and Cheddleton
- 27 MILES

Start: Oakamoor. Alternative starting points: Froghall or Cheadle.
Car Park: Oakamoor on former works site: or Froghall Canal Wharf.

The area around Cheadle does not have the dramatic vistas found in the northern tip of the county but there is a wide variety of scenery from wooded valleys to pastoral countryside. There is a wide choice of byways ideal for leisurely cycling. The total distance of the ride might easily be shortened by turning back at any one of several points (see map). For railway enthusiasts, there are two Railway Centres along the route, at Chedderton and Foxfield.

GRADIENTS: The first half of the ride involves some strenuous climbs especially on leaving OAKAMOOR, from FROGHALL TO IPSTONES and through BASFORD GREEN. The latter half of the ride is relatively easy.

Miles.	Places and route itinerary.	Information and Points of Interest.
	CHEADLE (See note a)	EC: Wed. MD: Fri. Sh. T. C. Cyc. Old Market Town. Ancient houses and inns. Tudor Houses in High Street. RC Church.
	OAKAMOOR. Cross Bridge and turn L at Cricketer's Arms: climb steeply and continue on hilly byroad through wooded country to:	PM. T. Site of Copper and Brass Foundry. Atlantic cable was made here. See Ride No.6.
2.5	**WHISTON.** At T junc L (sp A52 Stoke) descend steeply to:	Small village on hillside above Churnet Valley. Sharp bends on descent, care required.
1	**FROGHALL.** At foot of hill, turn R (sp B5053 Ipstones): climb steeply at times to outskirts of:	Canal Wharf (see Ride No.4) Towpath leads to CONSALL FORGE Picturesque location in Churnet Valley.

Miles	Places and route itinerary.	Information and Points of Interest.
1.5	**IPSTONES.** Turn L (sp Leisure Drive) and continue on narrow byroad and descend into wooded valley; continue along picturesque byroad; at T junc turn L and then climb steeply through:	(See Ride No.4) Belmont Hall; Chapel House, 1789 on L. Path on L to Devil's Staircase, steep descent into Churnet Valley (also see above under FROGHALL).
2.5	**BASFORD GREEN.** Continue ahead and fork L; continue past CHEDDLETON RAILWAY CENTRE (see note b) continue ahead to T junc (A520); and turn L and climb through:	Farming hamlet in secluded countryside. Hilly lanes. Steam Railway Centre and Museum. Cafe.
2	**CHEDDLETON.** Continue to climb and in 1.5m shortly after main road bends to L, turn L on byroad (Folly Lane); continue to T junc and turn L to:	Church, 13-15 cent. Old cross shaft, Stocks. Flint Mill, Water Wheels.
3.5	**CONSALL.** At entrance to village, turn sharp R (see note c); continue to T junc (A520); turn L and in 400 yds turn R on byroad (sp Dilhorne); continue to X rds (A52); continue str ahead on byroad; in half-mile bear L and then descend to outskirts of:	Quiet farming village at end of cul-de-sac. Old Hall, Nature Park. Mill. Care when crossing main road. Vision restricted.
3.5	**DILHORNE.** Turn L (sp Cheadle) and continue ahead; bear R and continue to:	Foxfield Railway Centre on R. Church: 13-15th cent.
2	**BROOKHOUSES.** At X rds (junc A521) continue str ahead (sp Draycott) and in half-mile turn L (sp Huntley); continue on narrow byroads to:	Group of cottages around junc with Cheadle-Longton road. Quiet back road.
2	**HUNTLEY.** Turn L and pass under bridge continue to T junc (A522); turn L into:	Hamlet hidden from traffic on A522.

Miles.	Places and route itinerary.	Information and Points of Interest.
1	**MOBBERLEY.** In 200 yds turn R (sp Freehay); climb for half-mile then fork L to:	Small village on Cheadle-Uttoxeter road.
1.5	**FREEHAY.** Cont str ahead to T junc (B 5032) turn L and imm turn R: continue to T junc (B5417): turn R and continue past:	Quiet lanes through open country.
2.5	**HAWKSMOOR NATURE RE-SERVE.** Continue ahead and descend into:	Bird Sanctuary (NT) 207 acres. Nature Trails.
1.5	OAKAMOOR (See note d).	

NOTES.
(a) If a start is made from CHEADLE, the B5417 should be taken and the main route joined on the approach to HAWKSMOOR NATURE RESERVE.
(b) a byroad on the L immediately after the RAILWAY CENTRE, leads direct to the A520 but omits the village of CHEDDLETON.
(c) Optional extension of the ride from CONSALL: turn L through village to NATURE PARK. From here, a path leads to CONSALL FORGE (see above). 2 miles return.

Members of the South Pennine Road Club on a ride through the Churnet Valley (Ride No.6)

29

RIDE NO.6
CHURNET VALLEY, ALTON, CROXDEN ABBEY and WEAVER HILLS - 24.5 MILES

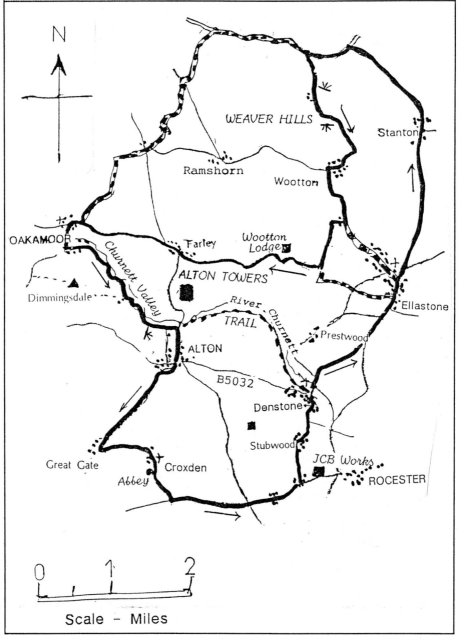

N

WEAVER HILLS

Stanton

Ramshorn

Wootton

OAKAMOOR

Farley

Wootton Lodge

Churnett Valley

Dimmingsdale

ALTON TOWERS

Ellastone

River Churnett

TRAIL

Prestwood

ALTON

B5032

Denstone

Stubwood

Great Gate

Croxden

Abbey

JCB Works

ROCESTER

0 1 2

Scale – Miles

RIDE NO. 6
CHURNET VALLEY, ALTON, CROXDEN ABBEY and WEAVER HILLS
- 24.5.MILES

Start: Oakamoor, on the B5417, 3 miles east of Cheadle.
Car Park: Oakamoor Country Park.

The first few miles are through the delightful Churnet Valley. After climbing to ALTON the route diverts through open country to the ruins of Croxden Abbey which nestles in a sheltered valley. A byways route to Denstone avoids the B5031 which is often busy with traffic travelling to and from Alton Towers. From Ellastone, there is a recommended diversion which climbs to Stanton and over the Weaver Hills from which on a clear day the view extends to the Malvern Mills. The return route passes through a wooded valley with the possibility of a glimpse of Wooton Lodge.

GRADIENTS: There is a short but very steep climb from the Churnet Valley to Alton village and another climb between Denstone and Ellastone. It is a long strenuous climb from Ellastone to Stanton and another from the A52 to the Weaver Hills from which there is a steep descent. After passing Wootton Lodge, there is a final climb to Farley.

Miles.	Places and route itinerary.	Information and Points of Interest.
	OAKAMOOR. Turn off the B5417 opposite the church and continue along a very narrow byroad: in half-mile fork L (see note a); and continue through valley passing (on R) Red House Cafe (see note b) in further 1m at T junc, turn very sharp R (see note c) and climb very steeply into:	PM. River Churnet. Country Park on site of former Copper and Brass Foundry. First Atlantic Cable made here in 1857-6. Delightful cycling route through wooded valley. Red House Cafe is popular with cyclists. View of Alton Towers (to L) and Alton Castle (ahead).
3	**ALTON.** Continue through village to T junc (B5032); turn R and in half-mile turn L on byroad; continue ahead for 1m to.	Sh. C. Alton Towers Pleasure Grounds, 1m N Alton Castle - school. Church 12 cent. Round House (Lock up) 15 cent. Trail to Denstone starts alongside bridge.
2	**GREAT GATE.** Turn L on narrow byroad to:	Farming hamlet in wooded valley.

Miles	Places and route itinerary.	Information and Points of Interest.
0.5	**CROXDEN ABBEY.** Continue ahead to T junc. turn L on undulating byroad and in 1.5m turn L to:	Ruins of Cistercian Abbey. c1253 in beautiful setting. JCB Works (half-mile east) are tastefully landscaped.
3	**STUBWOOD.** Descend to T junc. and turn L into:	Hamlet with cottages straggling along byroad.
1	**DENSTONE.** Turn R to T junc (B5031); turn L then turn R (B5032); cross bridge and climb for half-mile then desc to T junc (B5030) turn L to:	Small village. Church 1862. Denstone College. River Churnet. Cycle Trail from Alton ends at site of former railway station.
2.5	**ELLASTONE.** Continue through village (see note d) and turn R; desc and in half-mile turn L on narrow byroad; climb steeply at times to:	Attractive village was 'Hayslope' in the story of 'Adam Bede' by George Elliott. Inn was 'Donnisthorpe Arms'. River Churnet.
2.5	**STANTON.** Turn L and climb through open country: at T junc (A52) turn L; in half-mile turn L on field road; climb steeply at times to summit of:	Farming village. Earthworks in vicinity. Birthplace of Archbishop Sheldon.
3	**WEAVER HILLS.** Start steep descent with sharp corners; continue into:	Fine viewpoint which on a clear day extends to Malvern Hills.
1.5	**WOOTON.** Turn R then L; (see note e) descend for one-mile then turn R on byroad; in 1/2m turn R and desc; cont past:	Small village on lower slopes of Weaver Hills.
2	**WOOTTON LODGE.** Continue past lake and then climb; continue along boundary fence of ALTON TOWERS; at junction turn R through;	Home of founder JCB Tractors. Impressive building in secretive setting. Delightful cycling route through wooded valley.

Miles.	Places and route itinerary.	Information and Points of Interest.
2	FARLEY. Continue through village and turn L on byroad; desc to T junc (B5417); turn L across bridge into:	Manor House was a Youth Hostel in 1930s. Road through village often congested with traffic bound for ALTON TOWERS.
1.5	OAKAMOOR.	

NOTES:
(a) Byroad to R climbs for half-mile then a L turn leads to DIMMINGSDALE Youth Hostel.
(b) The track at the side of Red Hill Cafe leads to DIMMINGDALE Youth Hostel.
(c) The bridge at the foot of Alton Hill, is the start of a Cycling Trail along the former Churnet Valley railway track. This is a direct route to Denstone but it omits Alton village and Croxden Abbey.
(d) a left turn in ELLASTONE leads direct to WOOTTON LODGE but this omits WEAVER HILLS.
(e) From WOOTTON, there is an alternative route to OAKAMOOR via RAMSHORN (see map).

The ruins of Croxden Abbey rise above the byroad from Alton to Denstone.
(Ride No.6).

33

RIDE NO. 7
MILWICH, STONE, HILDERSTONE
and CHURCH LEIGH - 30 MILES

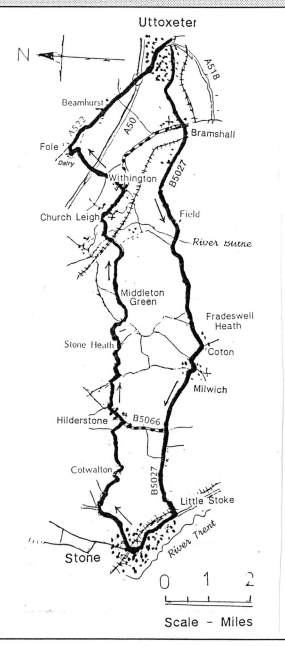

Scale - Miles

RIDE NO. 7
MILWICH, STONE, HILDERSTONE
and CHURCH LEIGH
- 30 MILES

Start: Uttoxeter Market Place. Alternative: Stone (see note a)
Car Park: Uttoxeter near church.

Almost the whole of this ride is along byways through farming countryside with its sounds and smells, very typical of central Staffordshire. The small bustling town of STONE is the halfway point on the ride and in both directions, the route passes through a succession of small villages most of which are devoted to dairy farming. Evidence of this will be found towards the end of the ride at the village of FOLE where there is a large dairy. The last few miles into UTTOXETER are along the A522 which was originally the busy A50 Derby - Stoke-on-Trent road but which is now diverted and which is crossed as the route enters UTTOXETER.

GRADIENTS: For the most part, the gradients throughout the ride are gently undulating. There are a few climbs eg. on leaving MILWICH and there is a descent on the approach to LITTLE STOKE. There is a climb after leaving the A520 beyond STONE and several climbs on the lanes around Hilderstone and into Church Leigh but none of them are really strenuous.

Miles.	Places and route itinerary.	Information and Points of Interest.
	UTTOXETER. Leave town centre by Smithfield Street (B5027 sp Stone) and continue out of town to:	EC: Thurs. MD: Thurs. Sh, T. Small industrial town. Associated with Dr. Samuel Johnson, sculpture in market Place. Racecourse 1m E. Church: 1830, 14c spire. Old Inns.
2.5	**BRAMSHALL.** Descend and cross level Xg then climb easily to open country; continue through:	Church. 1835 old glass.
2	**FIELD.** Cross bridge (River Blithe) and then continue on B5027; to:	Small farming village in the valley of River Blithe.
3	**COTON Turn.** Continue on B5027 and descend to:	Hamlet with some picturesque cottages.

Miles	Places and route itinerary.	Information and Points of Interest.
0.5	**MILWICH.** Continue ahead and in 1.5m at X roads (see note b) continue str ahead and descend; cross level Xg and at TR, turn R through:	Small pleasant village. Church 1792 has oldest bell in county.
4	**LITTLE STOKE.** Continue into:	Village an old main road through Trent Valley. Railway line is main west coast line London Euston to Glasgow.
1	**STONE.** Turn L then R (care required) and follow one-way system around town centre; leave by A520; in 11/2m at X rds, turn R (care when turning) as visibility is restricted); in half-mile turn R to:	EC: Thurs. MD: Alt Tues. Small industrial town in Trent Valley. St, Michael's Church. 1753. mausoleum of Admiral Earl St. Vincent. Priory remains. Old Inns associated with Hansom cab. 2 miles N is Downs Banks donated to National Trust.
2.5	**COTWALTON.** Climb through hamlet and continue on narrow byroad; in one-mile at T junc (B5066) turn R on byroad to:	Farming hamlet, hidden amongst lanes, Large farmhouse in derelict condition.
1.5	**HILDERSTONE.** At T junc, turn L past church; in half-mile turn R (Hall lane); climb past Hall and in 1m at T junc turn R; continue through:	Small village on B5066. Church: 1833 Romanesque. Picturesque lane route.
2	**STONE HEATH.** Fork L and continue ahead to:	Straggling village at heart of web of byroads.
1.5	**MIDDLETON GREEN.** Fork R and in 1m fork L on narrow byroad; desc to T junc and turn L across level crossing; cross bridge (River Blithe) into:	T. Quiet peaceful country byroads with very little traffic.
2	**LOWER LEIGH.** Turn R and climb to:	Pleasant hamlet with some picturesque cottages.

Miles.	Places and route itinerary.	Information and Points of Interest.
1	**CHURCH LEIGH.** At T junc turn R then L and continue to:	Church, 1846. glass. tomb.
1	**WITHINGTON.** Turn L then fork L (sp Fole); desc and pass under bridge (A50); descend and cross bridge (River Tean) and imm turn L past Dairy into:	Small village. (see note c)
1.5	**FOLE.** At T junc (A522, old A50) turn R and after short climb, continue through:	Small village now bypassed by A50.
1.5	**BEAMHURST.** Continue ahead and cross bridge (A50); at Tr fork R and continue into:	Hamlet with few picturesque cottages. River Tean.
2.5	**UTTOXETER.**	

NOTES:
(a) STONE is a convenient alternative starting point.
(b) The ride may be shortened by 8 miles by turning R on B5066 and rejoining main route at HILDERSTONE but this omits STONE.
(c) From WITHINGTON, there is an alternative route back to UTTOXETER via BRAMSHALL (see map).

A black and white half timbered cottage one of many similar cottages seen in Central Staffordshire.

RIDE NO. 8
MARCHINGTON, TUTBURY, DUNSTALL, and NEWBOROUGH - 32.5 MILES

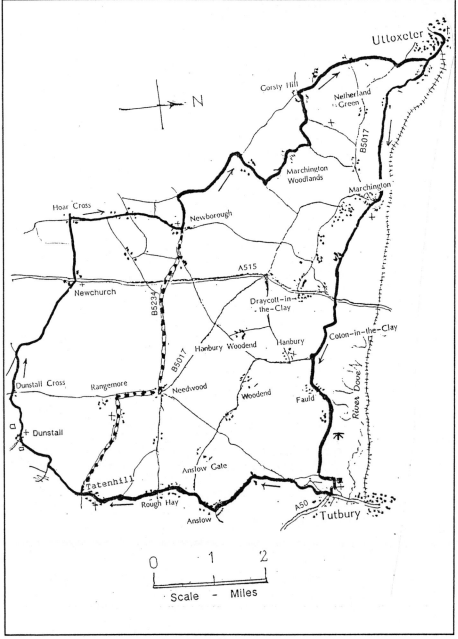

RIDE NO. 8
MARCHINGTON, TUTBURY, DUNSTALL,
and NEWBOROUGH.
- 32.5 MILES

Start: Uttoxeter Market Place. **Car Park:** Uttoxeter near Church.

To the east of UTTOXETER is a network of byways. The ride starts along the south side of the River Trent and from TUTBURY, a small town with an impressive church and ruins of a Saxon castle, the route turns southwards to TATENHILL and DUNSTALL. It then swings westwards across NEEDWOOD FOREST and through MARCHINGTON WOODLANDS. The scenery is not dramatic but it provides a base for some excellent cycling along quiet byroads through rural and well wooded countryside.

GRADIENTS: After an early climb beyond the entrance to the Race Course, the gradients are very easy to TUTBURY after which the route is undulating. Beyond DUNSTALL, the roads are more akin to a roller coaster but the climbs and descents are short.

Miles.	Places and route itinerary.	Information and Points of Interest.
	UTTOXETER. Leave Market Place by B5017; descend and cross railway bridge then turn L (Wood Lane); continue past entrance to Race Course and after short climb, continue along narrow byroad through open country to:	See Ride No 7.
3.5	**MARCHINGTON.** Turn R at grass triangle then turn L past church; after short climb continue through open country to staggered X rds (A515); turn L then R and continue ahead through:	Small village. Church 1744. Hall, 17 cent.
3	**COTON-in-the-CLAY.** Continue ahead and fork L (see note a) through:	Small village, black and white cottage.
1	**FAULD.** Continue ahead and after short climb turn L and then right into centre of:	Hall, Gypsum Mine. (See note a) View of Tutbury Castle ahead

Miles	Places and route itinerary.	Information and Points of Interest.
2	**TUTBURY.** At TR at top of High Street when A50 turns L; continue straight ahead (Ludgate St); in 1m turn L on byroad and again turn L (sp Anslow); turn L and continue on narrow byroad and climb to:	EC: Wed. Sh. PM. Ruins of 14 cent Castle, where Mary Queen of Scots was imprisoned. Church: c1100 has impressive west front. 'Dog & Partridge' Inn. Tudor Georgian houses.
2.5	**ANSLOW.** Turn R through village and in half-mile turn L to:	Small village near to Burton on Trent.
1	**ROUGH HAY (Acorn Inn)** at X rds (B5017) continue str ahead and desc through:	Hamlet at X rds.
1.5	**TATTENHILL.** At X rds continue str ahead; at next junc turn R (sp Dunstall); continue into:	Church: 13-15 cent: font. Griffin monument. (See note b)
1.5	**DUNSTALL.** Continue ahead to DUNSTALL CROSS and at X rds cont str ahead (sp Yoxall) and at next X rds turn R (sp Newchurch) continue to X rds (A515) at:	Picturesque estate village. Hall 19 cent. Church, 1853, spire. For several miles, there is a sequence of short climbs and decents.
3.5	**NEWCHURCH.** Continue str ahead (Brackenhurst Rd) and desc through woods to X rds at:	Care when crossing A515.
3	**HOAR CROSS.** Turn R and continue to:	(See Ride No.9).
1.5	**NEWBOROUGH.** Turn L and after short climb in further half-mile turn R on byroad (sp Marchington Woodlands); in 1.5m bear R and in 1m turn L; descend through woods and continue through:	Village at cross roads where B5234 dips into valley. Church 1901. Byroad now runs through open country on edge of Forest Banks.

Miles.	Places and route itinerary.	Information and Points of Interest.
4	MARCHINGTON WOOD-LANDS. Continue to T junc and turn L; at next T junc again turn L and continue to road junction at:	Small village in attractive wooded area.
1	GORSTY HILL. Turn R and in 2m at:	Cross roads at top of hill.
2	HIGHWOOD Cross Roads. Turn L (B5017); desc into:	
1.5	UTTOXETER.	

NOTES.
(a) A right turn leads to the village of HANBURY, the scene of a tragic incident during the 1939-45 war when a munitions store exploded causing a large loss of life and leaving a huge crater in the hillside above FAULD. The location can be found along a footpath from HANBURY village. Also see church 13 cent. Diversion 2m return.
(b) From TATENHILL, there is a slightly shorter alternative route, by turning R at the X rds and riding by RANGEMORE and NEEDWOOD and the B5234 to NEWBOROUGH.

The ancient Market Cross on the green at Abots Bromley. (Ride No.9)

41

RIDE NO. 9
ABBOTS BROMLEY, HAMSTALL RIDWARE
and BLITHBRIDGE. - 32.5 MILES

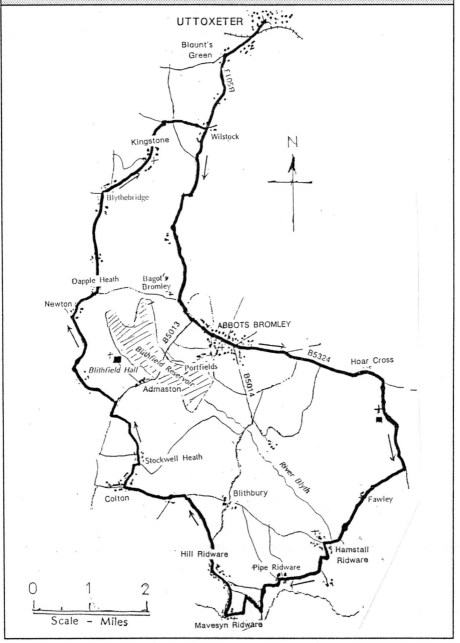

UTTOXETER

Blount's
Green

B5013

Kingstone   Wilstock

N

Blythebridge

Dapple Heath   Bagot's
Bromley

Newton   ABBOTS BROMLEY

B5013   B5324   Hoar Cross

Blithfield Reservoir
Blithfield Hall   Portfields   B5014
Admaston

Stockwell Heath

River Blyth

Colton   Blithbury   Fawley

Hamstall
Ridware

Hill Ridware
Pipe Ridware

0   1   2

Scale — Miles

Mavesyn Ridware

RIDE NO. 9
ABBOTS BROMLEY,
HAMSTALL RIDWARE
and BLITHBRIDGE
- 32.5 MILES

Start: UTTOXETER (Market Place)
Car Park: Near church.

A few miles to the south of Uttoxeter is the village of ABBOTS BROMLEY, the scene of an annual Horn Dance held on the Monday immediately following the 4th September. It is a unique event and worth including in this ride. At other times, the horns can be seen in St. Nicholas's church. On the return ride, the peaceful Ridware group of villages can be visited.

GRADIENTS:
After an initial climb from Uttoxeter to Willstock, the gradients are very comfortable with a final climb from Blithbridge through Kingstone.

Miles.	Places and route itinerary.	Information and Points of Interest.
	UTTOXETER. Leave by A518, cross level crossing and climb to:	See Ride No.7.
1	**BLOUNT'S GREEN.** Turn L (B5013) and climb to:	Small hamlet, suburb of UTTOXETER.
1.5	**WILLSTOCK.** Continue ahead to:	Pleasant road through woodlands, part of Bagot's Bromley estate.
3	**BAGOTS BROMLEY.** Continue str ahead into:	Ancient oaks.
1.5	**ABBOTS BROMLEY.** Continue through village and turn L (B5234) (see note a) in 1m fork R on byroad;continue to outskirts of:	EC: Wed. PM Butter Cross. Old Inns and houses. St. Nicholas' Church - horns. Annual Horn Dance on first Monday after 4th September. Manor House.
3	**HOARCROSS.** Turn R past Hoar Cross church; in 1.5m turn R on byroad; continue past:	Church: 1876, impressive, built by widow of Lord of Manor as memorial to her husband. Very dark inside but lighting available. Hall; home of Mynell-Ingram family.

Miles	Places and route itinerary.	Information and Points of Interest.
2	FAWLEY (Farm). Continue str ahead and in 1m fork R; cross bridge (River Blithe) and turn R into:	Road is shown as 'No Through Road' to traffic but available to cyclists.
1.5	HAMSTALL RIDWARE. Retrace route and continue ahead; in half-mile fork R and in 1m turn L into:	Church, 12 -15 cent. Wall paintings. Screens, tombs. Manor House. 16 cent. fine gateway.
2	PIPE RIDWARE. In half-mile turn L and at junc with B5014, turn R then turn L to:	Church, 1842 Norman font. Farming village.
1.5	MAVESYN RIDWARE. Continue through village and rejoin B5014; turn L through:	Church; 1782, Tower 15 cent, tombs, floor tiles. Hall: early 18 cent. Manor gatehouse, 15-16 cent.
1	HILL RIDWARE. In 1m fork L on byroad and at T junc turn L towards:	Unspectacular village.
2.5	CALTON. At entrance to village, turn R; in half-mile at T junc turn L through:	Church :18 cent.
1	STOCKWELL HEATH. Continue ahead to T junc (B5014) and turn R; in 200 yds turn L; in 1.5m turn R into:	Farming village. Blithfield Hall on R.
2	NEWTON. Continue ahead through:	Farms.
0.5	DAPPLE HEATH. Continue to:	Farming hamlet: quiet country lanes.
1.5	BLYTHEBRIDGE. Turn R and after short climb continue to:	PM. Pleasant location.

Miles.	Places and route itinerary.	Information and Points of Interest.
1.5	**KINGSTONE.** Climb through village then turn R; at X rds continue ahead to X rds at:	Farming village.
1.5	**WILLSTOCK.** Turn L (B5013); retrace outward route; at T junc (A518); turn R through:	PM.
1.5	**BLOUNTS GREEN.** Retrace outward route and descend into:	
1	**UTTOXETER.**	

NOTES.

(a) The ride may be shortened by continuing from ABBOTS BROMLEY along the B5014 and immediately after crossing the River Blithe turn R and join the main route on the approach to STOCKWELL HEATH but this omits HOAR CROSS and the RIDWARE villages.

The Horn Dance held annually at Abbots Bromley. (Ride No.9).

RIDE NO. 10
CANNOCK CHASE and the TRENT VALLEY
- 23 MILES

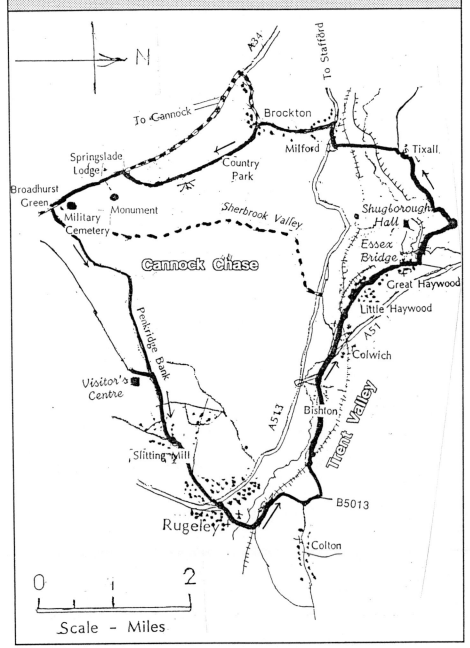

N

To Stafford

A34

To Cannock

Brockton

Springslade Lodge

Milford

Tixall

Country Park

Broadhurst Green

Monument

Military Cemetery

Sherbrook Valley

Shugborough Hall

Essex Bridge

Cannock Chase

Great Haywood

Little Haywood

A51

Penkridge Bank

Colwich

Visitor's Centre

A513

Bishton

Trent Valley

Slitting Mill

B5013

Rugeley

Colton

0   1   2

Scale - Miles

RIDE NO. 10
CANNOCK CHASE
and the
TRENT VALLEY
- 23 MILES

Start: Milford on A513, 3 1/2 miles east of STAFFORD or alternatively, RUGELEY.
Car Park: Adjoining green off A518.

The route first climbs to the village of BROCKTON where it turns to the high ground of Cannock Chase Country Park. There is an excellent cycling route across the Chase and after visiting the Military Cemetery, it turns back to the outskirts of RUGELEY. The final miles are through quiet byroads of the Trent Valley.

GRADIENTS:
The first four miles are strenuous but after Broadhurst Green, it is very easy with some long descents. The return from the outskirts of RUGELEY is also very easy.

Miles.	Places and route itinerary.	Information and Points of Interest.
	MILFORD. From Green, take byroad south and climb to:	Sh. C - Little Fawn Restaurant.
1.5	**BROCKTON.** (See note a). At small green turn L and imm. left again (Sign Cannock Chase Brockton); climb steeply for half-mile and enter CANNOCK CHASE COUNTRY PARK; climb to highest point of CHASE; continue to T junc and turn L to:	18 cent hall. Chetwynd Arms also 18 cent. Views across CHASE.
2.5	**SPRINGSLADE LODGE..** Continue ahead to:	C (Cl Mon and Fri) Katryn Monument (on L). Commemorates death of Polish Serviceman in 1940 in Katryn Forest.
1	**MILITARY CEMETERY.** Continue ahead to X rds at:	Graves of Servicemen including Germans from First World War.
0.5	**BROADHURST GREEN.** Turn left (see note b) and continue through forest; in 3m descend Penkridge Bank and turn R to:	Road runs through Forest but there are occasional breaks in the trees giving some extensive views.

Miles	Places and route itinerary.	Information and Points of Interest.
3.0	**FOREST VISITORS CENTRE.** Retrace route to T junc and turn R; descend to outskirts of:	Information Centre and Exhibition.
2.0	**RUGELEY.** At TL at X rds (junc (A51), continue straight ahead (Church Street); continue to T junc; turn R to TR and turn L (sp B5013 Uttoxeter); cross bridges (canal and River Trent); continue ahead and pass under railway bridge; turn L and continue for 1.5 miles then turn L on byroad (sp Bishton), pass under railway bridge and continue through:	EC: Wed. MD: Thurs. Sat. Sh. C. Old church, 12-13 cent (in ruins). small industrial town in Trent Valley.
4.0	**BISHTON.** Continue to T junc (A51) and turn R; in half-mile turn left through:	Hall 18 cent. Now a school. Care when crossing A51.
1.0	**COLWICH.** Pass under railway bridge and continue through:	Small village now bypassed by A51, Church: 13-14 cent. Tombs. St Benedict's Priory.
0.5	**LITTLE HAYWOOD.** Climb for half -mile then descent into:	Sh.
1.0	**GREAT HAYWOOD.** In centre of village turn L on narrow street, (see note c); pass under low railway bridge and cross canal bridge to:	EC: Tues. Sh. Pleasant village now bypassed by A51.
0.5	**ESSEX BRIDGE.** Ride along bridle road into:	Rivers Trent and Sow join on R. Bridge has 14 arches and gives direct access to SHUGBOROUGH PARK and HALL.
	SHUGBOROUGH PARK. Retrace route across ESSEX BRIDGE to:	Seat of Anson family. Fine collection of paintings. Attractive gardens and grounds. Triumphal arch.

Miles.	Places and route itinerary.	Information and Points of Interest.
1.5	**GREAT HAYWOOD.** Turn L; in 150 yds at TR turn L; pass under railway bridge and cross canal bridge; continue on winding by-roads to:	See above.
2.0	**TIXALL.** At grass triangle turn L and in half-mile cross canal then River Sow and railway then turn R (sp Stafford); at T junc turn R to:	Mary Queen of Scots was once imprisoned in the Hall. Gatehouse c1580.
2.0	**MILFORD.**	

NOTES:

(a) From BROCKTON, there is an alternative route: continue straight ahead and at junc with A34, turn L and in 150 yds again turn L and climb steeply then continue ahead to SPRINGSLADE LODGE where join main route. Distance same as main route.

(b) From BROADHURST GREEN, there is an alternative but longer route to RUGELEY via GREENHEATH and WANDON (See Map).

(c) The diversion to ESSEX BRIDGE and the ride through SHUGBOROUGH PARK are optional but strongly recommended. The bridleway (signed) gives access to the main car park where cycles may be left under supervision. Bicycles are not permitted within the gardens.

A short diversion in the village of Great Haywood leads to the Essex Bridge which gives access to SHUGBOROUGH HALL and PARK. (Ride No. 10).

RIDE NO. 11
WOODSEAVES, SHEBDON, and ECCLESHALL
- 27.5 MILES

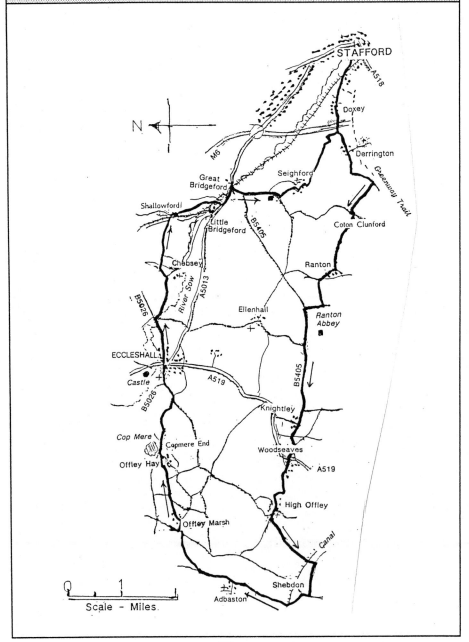

Scale - Miles

50

RIDE NO. 11
WOODSEAVES, SHEBDON
and ECCLESHALL
- 27.5 MILEs

Start: Stafford, Broad Eye Traffic Roundabout.

Car Park: Various Car Parks around Town Centre.

Almost the whole of this ride to the west of Stafford is along quiet byroads through open farming countryside. The route rarely touches a main road so it would be an ideal ride for a holiday weekend. Whilst there are few high spots it is a very pleasant cycling route.

GRADIENTS.
The gradients throughout the ride are very easy with no hills of any consequence.

Miles.	Places and route itinerary.	Information and Points of Interest.
	STAFFORD. Turn along Doxey Road; cross bridge (River Sow) and at TR fork L; cross railway bridge) then continue through:	EC: Wed. MD: Tues, Sat, Inf. BR. interesting old town with many narrow streets. Much of the central area is now pedestrianised. High House, Swan Hotel. St. Mary's Church. Stafford Castle (1 1/2m W).
1	**DOXEY.** Cross Bridge (M6) and continue through:	Former village now a residential suburb of Stafford. Start of Greenwood Trail Cycling Route. off the Drive. See Ride 12.
0.5	**ASTON.** Continue ahead through outskirts of:	Hall. Farms.
1	**DERRINGTON.** In half-mile turn R on narrow byroad; in half-mile at:	Centre of village along byroad to L. Also access point to Greenwood Cycling Trail.
1	**COTON CLANFORD.** turn L then R continuing on narrow byroad; in 1 mile at T junc, turn R through:	Very narrow traffic free byroads excellent for leisurely cycling

Miles	Places and route itinerary.	Information and Points of Interest.
1.5	**RANTON.** Continue through village and turn L on byroad; in half-mile at T junc turn R to T junc (B5405) turn L through open country; continue through.	Small village of old and new cottages. Church 13 cent. Ranton Abbey, 15 cent tower.
3	**KNIGHTLEY.** Continue ahead and on approach to:	
1	**WOODSEAVES** Fork R (Dickey Lane); at X rds (A519) continue str ahead; continue to:	Sh. Small village on A519 Newport - Eccleshall road. Care when crossing.
1	**HIGH OFFLEY** After church at X rds turn L on narrow byroad (no sp) cross canal and in half-mile at T junc turn R (no sp) in further half-mile at T junc turn R) (no sp) through:	Small village in open country. Church: 12-17 cent. Narrow twisting byway. Shropshire Union Canal.
2	**SHEBDON.** Continue ahead and pass under canal bridge; continue to road junction at:	PM.
1.5	**ADBASTON.** Continue ahead and in half-mile turn R (Lerridge Lane); in 1m at T junc, turn L and in half-mile turn R (no sp) to:	Church: 15 cent. Norman windows. Mediaeval tombs.
2	**OFFLEYMARSH.** At green, fork L on narrow byroad; in 1/2m at T junc turn left through:	A few cottages clustered round a village green. Lovely traffic free country byway.
1	**OFFLEYHAY.** Descend to T junc: turn R through:	
0.5	**COPMERE END.** Continue ahead and climb to:	Cop Mere small lake on L. PM.
1	**ELFORD HEATH.** At green fork L and descend to T junc (B5026); turn R into:	Pleasant village green.

Miles.	Places and route itinerary.	Information and Points of Interest.
0.5	ECCLESHALL. At X rds continue str ahead in 1m cross bridge (River Sow) and turn R on narrow byroad; at X rds continue ahead on narrow byroad descend to T junc and turn R; cross bridges (Meece Brook and railway) to:	EC: Wed. MD: Fri. and alt Mon. Sh. C. Church, c.1500. Fine tower. Monuments to Bishops of Lichfield. Castle ruins. The Byroad is grass grown and very narrow but it us all rideable.
3	SHALLOWFORD. Continue ahead and in 1.5 miles cross bridges (River Sow and railway); at T junc (A5013) turn L to:	Isaac Walton's cottage. Attractive thatched, black and white half timbered. Angling Museum. Herb Garden.
2	GREAT BRIDGEFORD. On approach to railway bridge, turn R (B5405) and in half-mile turn L on byroad (sp Seighford); after passing Hall on R, turn L into:	Care when turning off A5103. Attractive black and white half timbered Hall, 16 cent.
1.5	SEIGHFORD. Continue through village and in 1.5m turn L across bridge (M6) through:	Church, 12-15 cent. Tombs. 17 cent pulpit.
1.5	DOXEY. Retrace outward route into:	
1.5	STAFFORD.	

A picturesque cottage at Shallowford was once the home of Isaac Walton, the famous angler. (Ride No.11).

RIDE NO. 12
PENKRIDGE, BREWOOD and THE GREENWAY
- 33 MILES

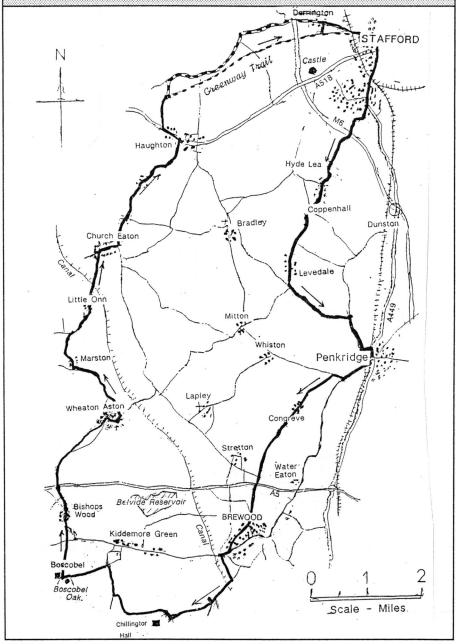

RIDE NO. 12
PENKRIDGE, BREWOOD
and THE GREENWAY
- 33 MILES

Start: Stafford, Wolverhampton Road.
Car Park: Various Car Parks in Town Centre.

To the south west of STAFFORD, the rich farming countryside is crossed by a network of quiet byways which are ideal for leisurely cycling and on which little traffic will be encountered. The highlight of the ride is a visit to BREWOOD, an ancient place with numerous points of interest. The return is along the, The Greenway, a former railway track converted to a cycleway.

GRADIENTS. The gradients are gently undulating throughout the ride, the altitude rarely exceeding 100 ft.

Miles.	Places and route itinerary.	Information and Points of Interest.
	STAFFORD. Leave town centre by A449 (Wolverhampton Road); cross railway bridge and in half-mile turn right (sp Hyde Lea); imm. turn left and continue through residential area; pass under bridge (M6) and climb through:	See Ride No.11.
2	**HYDE LEA.** Continue ahead through:	Small residential suburb of Stafford.
0.5	**COPPENHALL.** Continue on quiet byroad through open countryside to:	Small village. Church; c.1220.
2	**LEVEDALE.** Continue ahead (sp Penkridge) and descend; turn L under railway bridge to T junc (A449) ; turn R into:	Small farming village.

55

Miles	Places and route itinerary.	Information and Points of Interest.
2.5	**PENKRIDGE.** In centre of village turn R (sp Whiston); pass under railway bridge; in 1/2m at X rds turn R across Cuttlestone Bridge then turn left on byroad through:	Sh. Former village on A449 Stafford to Wolverhampton road developed in recent years. Inns. Church 13-16 cent. tombs. River Penk flows into the River Sow at Stafford.
1.5	**CONGREVE.** Continue to X rds at jun of:	Hamlet: Manor House and farm.
1.5	**A5** Continue ahead and in 1m turn right to:	<u>Care when crossing traffic usually heavy.</u>
1.5	**BREWOOD.** At Market Place continue straight ahead past church; bear left and after short descent continue to cross roads; turn right (sp Chillington); cross canal bridge and climb to cross roads; at Giffard's Cross, turn R on byroad (sp Chillington) continue to T junc at:	Sh. C. One time market town. Ancient village worth lengthy exploration. Church 13-14 cent. Old houses. Speedwell Castle, Gothic building. Priest's House. Hall. Tithe Barn. Shropshire Canal. Giffard's Cross, panther shot in 1513 with cross bow.
2	**CHILLINGTON HALL.** Turn R and in 1.5m turn L and climb to T junc near:	Hall, 1724 and 1789 Seat of Giffard family. Park by 'Capability Brown'. Hall open limited days.
2.5	**BOSCOBEL HOUSE.** Turn R and continue to:	Boscobel House where Charles 11 hid. Boscobel Oak in grounds.
1	**BISHOP'S WOOD.** Continue straight ahead and after short descent, climb to T junc (A5) at:	Road here runs along boundary with Shropshire. PM.
1	**IVETSY BANK.** Turn R and imm turn L on byroad continue ahead to:	Traffic usually heavy on A5. <u>Care required when crossing A5.</u>
1.5	**WHEATON ASTON.** Turn L in village (Marston Road) and continue to:	Sh. Small farming village. Byroad runs through open countryside.

Miles.	Places and route itinerary.	Information and Points of Interest.
1.5	**MARSTON.** Fork R and continue through:	Farming hamlet.
1.5	**LITTLE ONN.** Continue ahead, cross canal and continue to:	Black and White Hall. St. Edith's Well.
1.5	**CHURCH EATON.** At T junc, turn R through village and at church, turn L (sp Haughton) and continue through:	Church, 11 cent. Large village.
0.5	**APETON.** and:	Scattered village of farms.
0.5	**ALLIMORE GREEN** to:	
1	**HAUGHTON** At T junc (A518) turn left and in 400 yds turn right (sp Rantron, Station Road, in half-mile turn left through gate into Car Park at start of:	Sh. Church, 14-15 cent, Hall, 16 cent half timbered.
1	**GREENWAY CYCLE TRAIL.** See note a. Turn right under bridge and continue along TRAIL past: access point to:	
2	**DERRINGTON CAR PARK.** Continue ahead under bridge (M6) and in half-mile leave TRAIL and turn left on track to THE DRIVE: turn right to:	
2	**DOXEY.** At T junc, turn right and continue into:	
2	**STAFFORD.**	

NOTES.
(a) The GREENWAY Trail has a hard surface but the width of the riding area is narrow. There is insufficient width to permit passing other cyclists or pedestrians without dismounting. Horse riders use a separate strip, Alternative route via DERRINGTON.

RIDE NO. 13
AROUND LICHFIELD, ALREWAS, WHITTINGTON and WALL - 34.5 MILES

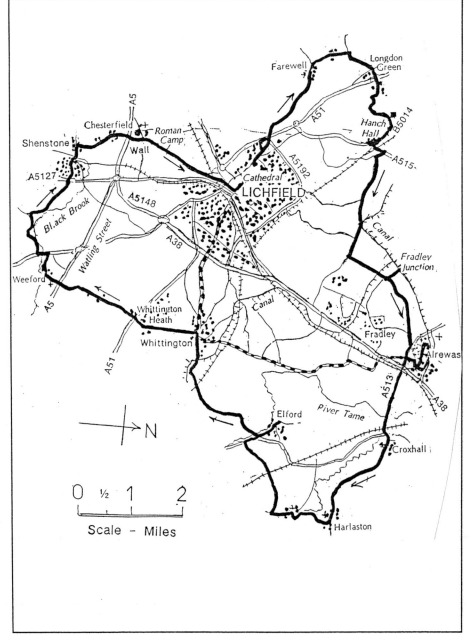

Scale - Miles

RIDE NO. 13
AROUND LICHFIELD, ALREWAS, WHITTINGTON and WALL.
- 34.5 MILES

Start: Lichfield Cathedral. **Car Park:** Lichfield Bird Street.

There is some delightful rural countryside around LICHFIELD. When planning cycling routes however, it is advisable so far as is possible to avoid the bypasses and other busy main roads which surround LICHFIELD. This recommended route can be divided into two loops by using a byroad between Whittington and the City centre (see map). The highspots of the ride include several picturesque villages - Longdon Green, Alrewas which has some attractive cottages; Elford and Weeford, which are hidden away from main road traffic along quiet byroads. Towards the end of the ride there is an opportunity to visit the Roman Station at Wall.

GRADIENTS: The byroad from Lichfield to Longdon Green involves several climbs and descents but the remainder of the ride is gently undulating.

Miles.	Places and route itinerary.	Information and Points of Interest.
	LICHFIELD. Leave by Beacon St. and at TR (near Safeways Store) continue ahead; in 200 yds turn L (Abnalls Lane); continue to T junc (A51); turn R and in 400 yds turn L on narrow byroad; continue ahead (several climbs and descents) to:	EC: Wed: MD: Fri., Sh. C. T. Cathedral, three prominent spires known as 'The Ladies of the Vale'. Chantrey's monument 'Sleeping Children'. Old houses. Bishop's Palace. Stowe Pool, picturesque. Dr. Samuel Johnson's birthplace. Care when crossing A51. Rural scenery, farming country.
2.5	**FAREWELL.** At grass triangle, turn R and continue to:	Farming village. Hall 18 cent. Church: c1745.
1.5	**LONGDON GREEN.** At X rds, continue straight ahead under bridge (A51) and at T junc (B5014) turn R; in half-mile opp Waterworks, turn L on narrow byroad; continue to T junc (A515) and turn L; cross rly bridge and in 250 yds turn R (Wood End Lane); in 2m turn L (sp Fradley Junction); in 1m cross canal bridge and at X rds turn L; at canal bridge turn L to:	Large green on old A51 (now bypassed). Hanch Hall. Care when turning across main road.

59

Miles	Places and route itinerary.	Information and Points of Interest.
5.5	**FRADLEY JUNCTION.** Retrace route to X rds and turn L; continue to T junc (A513); turn R and in 150 yds turn L into:	Junction of Trent & Mersey and Coventry Canals built by James Brindley. Boating centre.
2.5	**ALREWAS.** Turn L in centre of village, cross canal bridge and imm. turn R past church; continue alongside river, again cross canal and turn R; return to centre of village and retrace route to T junc. (A513) turn L; at TR continue ahead, cross bridge (A38) and at second TR continue ahead on A513 (sp Tamworth); in 1.5m pass under railway bridge and imm turn L; in 400 yds turn R to:	EC: Thurs. Sh. Picturesque village, attractive cottages some of them thatched. Church: 12 -15 cent. Font. Mill. Pleasant riverside. Places to picnic. Village is now bypassed by A513 as a result access and exit is not easy without cycling along a busy main road.
2.5	**CROXALL.** Continue through village to:	Church 13-15 cent. Curzon tombs. Monument by Chantry. Hall
1.5	**EDINGALE.** Continue through village and turn R; cross bridge and at T junc turn L and climb into:	Church, c1735.
1.5	**HARLASTON.** Turn R, continue past church and in 0.5m again turn R; continue to T junc (A513); turn R then fork L into:	Pleasant village. Church 1883 has half timbered belfry. RC Chapel. Haselour Hall, 16 cent. half timbered.
2.5	**ELFORD.** Continue into village then retrace route to T junc; turn R and in 200 yds again turn R cross bridge (River Tame) and continue on byroad through:	Beautiful village in wooded area: River Tame. St. Peter's church, alabaster tombs. Hall, moated. Picnic site on river bank.
2.5	**FISHERWICK.** Continue across level crossing to:	Farming hamlet. Main west coast line from London to Scotland.
1.0	**WHITTINGTON.** At X rds turn L (sp Hopwas); continue to T junc (A51) at:	Small pleasant village.
1.5	**WHITTINGTON HEATH.** Turn L and imm. turn R (sp Weeford); continue to X rds (Junc A5); continue str ahead and descend into:	Military Camp. firing range. Care when crossing A5, busy main road.

Miles.	Places and route itinerary.	Information and Points of Interest.
2.0	**WEEFORD.** Continue ahead to T junc (A38); turn L, cross bridge (Black Brook) and imm turn R (sp Little Hay), continue through valley and at next junction turn R (sp Shenstone); continue to X rds (junc A5127) continue str ahead into:	Small picturesque village. Church, 1800 has some French glass. <u>Care when turning R across dual carriageway.</u> Picturesque lane route through woods. <u>Care when crossing A5127.</u>
2.5	**SHENSTONE.** At T junc turn R into cul-de-sac at end of which dismount and walk along foot path; continue through village and at T junc (Railway Inn); turn L; cross railway bridge and in half-mile turn R on byroad; continue through:	Church: 1853. Bull's Head Inn, 18 cent. Footpath leads to pleasant corner of village.
1.5	**CHESTERFIELD.** Continue ahead and at X rds (junc A5); continue straight ahead into:	Farming hamlet.
1	**WALL.** At X rds, turn L then R; in village turn R (sp Lichfield) and at T junc, turn R; in 200 yds turn L; descend to T junc (A38); turn L and at TR turn R into:	Site of 'Letocetum' Roman Station. near junction of Watling and Ryykneld Streets. Museum. Baths and Villas.
2.5	**LICHFIELD.**	

A short diversion on Ride No.13 leads to the Fradley Canal Junction.

RIDE NO. 14
WOMBOURN CYCLE TRAIL, KINVER and ENVILLE
- 29.5 MILES

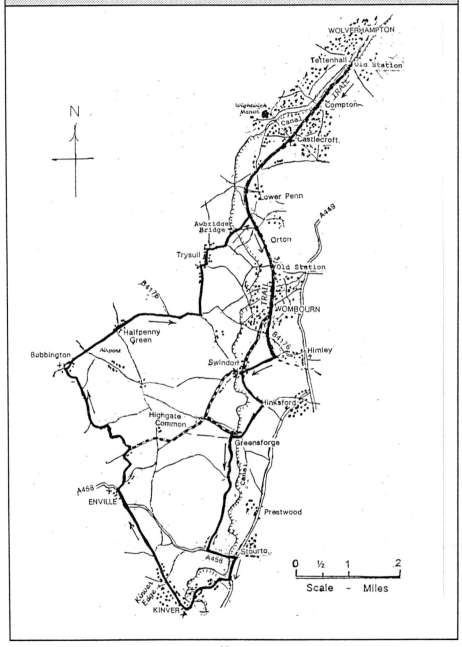

RIDE NO. 14
WOMBOURN CYCLE TRAIL, KINVER and ENVILLE.
- 29.5 MILES

Start: Tettenhall Old Station off A41, 1 1/2 miles NW of Wolverhampton.
Car Park: Tettenhall Old Station.

This ride on the edge of the Black Country, starts along a Trail which first runs through Valley Park and then continues along the Wombourn Railway Path. From Himley, the route turns south along byroads which link some small villages and eventually turns into Kinver. The return to Tettenhall is mostly along traffic free byroads through Enville, Bobbington and Trysull. The Trail is then rejoined for the last four miles back to Tettenhall.

GRADIENTS. The first seven miles along the Trail are very easy. For the most part the byroads from Himley to Kinver and the return through Bobbington are gently undulating but there are a few short hills, none of them too strenuous.

Miles.	Places and route itinerary.	Information and Points of Interest.
	TETTENHALL Old Station. From Car Park, join TRAIL southward; cross bridges and continue past access point at:	Car Park. Toilets. Rangers Information Office. The bridges cross the Semstow Brook and the Staffordshire & Worcester Canal (Warren Truss Girder Bridge known as 'Meccano Bridge' next bridge at Compton crosses the A454 Bridgenorth Road.
1.5	**CASTLECROFT.** Pass through gate and continue along TRAIL to:	A slope on left leads to a road to Wolverhampton (alternative starting point to ride) Road across the bridge leads to WIGHTWICK MANOR (NT). 1.5 miles return. Picnic sites alongside the Trail.
3.0	**WOMBOURN Old Station.** In further one-mile the Trail climbs to cross an accommodation road at the outskirts of:	Tea Rooms. Car Park.
1.0	**WOMBOURN.** (See note a) Continue on TRAIL and in one mile turn through Car Park at site of:	Sh. Church 1867, tower and spire are 14-15 cent.
1.0	**HIMLEY STATION.** Leave TRAIL and turn right on by-road to:	

63

Miles	Places and route itinerary.	Information and Points of Interest.
1.0	SWINDON. Turn left and in 150 yds turn left; (see note b); continue alongside canal and at X rds turn right; in half-mile again turn right to:	Staffordshire & Worcester Canal.
2.0	GREENSFORGE. Cross canal and turn left; in 100 yds turn left (Greenforge Lane); (see note c); in 3 miles at T junc (A458) turn left; descend, cross bridge into outskirts of:	Pleasant area alongside canal. Wooded area alongside canal.
3.0	STOURTON. At T junc (A449) turn right on duel carriageway; in half-mile turn right on byroad to:	Remains of Castle. The A449 is very busy. Care required when crossing duel carriageway. Care also required when crossing into road to Dunsley.
1.0	DUNSLEY. Descend and cross bridge into:	Small farming hamlet.
1.0	KINVER. Continue through village and after short climb, continue through:	Sh. Cafe. (Cl Mon). Old houses. Church 14-15 cent. Kinver Edge (NT) rock formations. climb to summit for view.
0.5	POTTER'S CROSS. Continue ahead to junction with A458; turn left through.	Wooded area.
2.0	ENVILLE. In centre of village turn right on byroad (sp Swinton) and in half-mile turn left on narrow byroad (sp Bobbington); in half-mile at T junc. turn right (so sp); and in 200 yds turn left on narrow byroad (no sp); in one-mile turn left (no sp) and in half-mile turn right, (sp Bobbington); in one-mile turn left (Church Lane) to:	Church, tombs. Hall 18 cent. Although on a main road it is an attractive village with a green. The route follows narrow traffic byroads which are ideal for leisurely cycling. Few of the junctions are signposted so it is necessary to follow a map or these directions carefully. Rural farming area.
4.5	BOBBINGTON. At T junc turn R and continue to:	Church 12 cent. Tombs. Parish chest. Yew.
1.5	HALFPENNY GREEN. Continue ahead through village and in 1m join B4176; descend and at X rds in half-mile turn L (sp Trysull); continue through:	Aerodrome.

Miles.	Places and route itinerary.	Information and Points of Interest.
3.0	**TRYSULL** At T junc (imm after church) turn right and imm fork right descend and cross canal bridge after short climb, turn left (Union Lane); continue along narrow byroad and shortly before bridge; turn right on track; turn left on TRAIL; return past:	Pleasant village, Church 12 cent. Manor House. Picturesque stretch of Staffordshire & Worcester Canal.
3.0	**CASTLECROFT Access Point.** Retrace route along TRAIL to:	
1.5	**TETTENHALL Old Station.**	

NOTES.

(a) There is an alternative route to SWINDON, by leaving the TRAIL at this point. (see map).

(b) From SWINDON, there is an alternative route to GREENSFORGE (see map).

(c) The distance may be shortened by riding from GREENSFORGE direct to BOBBINGTON (see map) but this omits KINVER, one of the highlights of the Ride.

The Author at Tettenhall Old Station at the start of a ride along the Wombourn-Kingswinford Trail (Ride No.14).

DIMMINGSDALE.

Dimmingsdale Youth Hostel is in a delightful woodland setting in the hills above the Churnet Valley. The original hostel opened in 1941 was a wooded building but in recent years it has been rebuilt in brick. It has always been a self cookers hostel.

There are two approaches: by a hilly road from Oakamoor or by turning off the byroad through the Churnet Valley at the Red House Cafe and climbing a woodland track. 20% of bednights are attributed to cyclists and perhaps surprisingly in view of its remote location, many of them are from other countries. The cycle shed is open so locking of machines is advised. There is a small store and adequate cooking facilities.

It is a cosy hostel especially in the winter. From the windows there is a view of Alton Towers across the valley.

The original Youth Hostel at Dimmingsdale was housed in huts but the present hostel was specially built.

MEERBROOK.

The small self cooking hostel at Meerbrook was formerly the village school which closed in 1978 when it was expected that the village would be submerged when the Tittesworth Reservoir was being extended. This did not happen and soon afterwards, the building became a youth hostel. The hostel which has a family room is now a listed building. Much of the maintenance has been carried out by YHA groups.

It is becoming increasingly popular with local cycling groups and by riders on the Lands End to John o' Groats trip. Locally it is convenient for the Roaches area.

Meerbrook Youth Hostel, originally a school, its 'life' was reprieved when plans for the extension of the nearby Tittesworth Reservoir were finalised.

ILAM HALL.

Ilam Hall is one of the YHA's most majestic hostels. The approach from the village is along a drive through the park then there is a 'surprise' view of the hostel which is a National Trust property. The main entrance is imposing and opens into an entrance hall from which steps lead to the main floor. There is a total of 148 beds which includes some Family Accommodation.

There is a Games Room. TV Room and a peaceful Quiet Room.
There is a good cycle store in the arch way at the side of the main building.

GRADBACH MILL.

Gradbach Mill is tucked away in a secluded valley on the Cheshire side of the border. A surfaced road leads to the hostel from a byroad which descends from Flash. It is well situated as a link hostel for cyclists touring in the north east tip of Staffordshire.

It is a solid looking building typical of the mills of the 18th and 19th cent. It has been little changed externally but inside it has been well fitted out to modern YHA standards. The cycle shed is in an annex that was once the Mill Owner's house.

In the centre of the ancient village of Breewood, is a Gothic building known as Speedwell Castle. Ride No. 12.

CYCLING GUIDES by ARNOLD ROBINSON.

All contain Route Itineraries, Route Maps, details of Gradients and Surfaces, Touring Information, Points of Interest, Viewpoints and Scenic Attractions, Location of accommodation, Youth Hostels, camp sites, places to eat and cycle repairers. The suggested cycling routes may be ridden as 'day rides' or linked together to form an on-going tour.

CYCLING Around CASTLETON and the Hope Valley.

CYCLING Around MATLOCK.

CYCLING Around BUXTON

CYCLING Around CHESTERFIELD.

CYCLING Around LEICESTERSHIRE & RUTLAND

CYCLING Around LINCOLNSHIRE.

CYCLING Around NORTHUMBERLAND

CYCLING Around THE LAKE DISTRICT.

CYCLING Around the NORTH YORKSHIRE MOORS - ten routes which provide an on-going tour.

CYCLING Around STAFFORDSHIRE

CYCLING Around the COTSWOLDS

CYCLING Around the YORKSHIRE WOLDS.

CYCLING Around DERBY

CYCLING Around THE ISLE OF MAN

CYCLING around the PEAK DISTRICT - contains eleven routes which may be ridden individually or linked together to form an 'on-going' tour. Details are also given of the popular off-highway Trails.

CYCLING around SHEFFIELD - nine routes in Sheffield's 'Golden Frame.'

CYCLING around HARTINGTON -touring information and route itineraries.

CYCLING around BAKEWELL - touring information and route itineraries.

CYCLING around ASHBOURNE - touring information and route itineraries.

CYCLING in DERBYSHIRE - eleven of the best cycling routes, mainly in the southern half of the country.

CYCLING in NOTTINGHAMSHIRE - twelve cycling routes which cover most of the county.

CYCLING around CHESHIRE - twelve routes.

OTHER JOHN MERRILL WALK BOOKS

CIRCULAR WALK GUIDES -
SHORT CIRCULAR WALKS IN THE PEAK DISTRICT - Vol. 1,2, 3 AND 9
CIRCULAR WALKS IN WESTERN PEAKLAND
SHORT CIRCULAR WALKS IN THE STAFFORDSHIRE MOORLANDS
SHORT CIRCULAR WALKS - TOWNS & VILLAGES OF THE PEAK DISTRICT
SHORT CIRCULAR WALKS AROUND MATLOCK
SHORT CIRCULAR WALKS IN "PEAK PRACTICE COUNTRY."
SHORT CIRCULAR WALKS IN THE DUKERIES
SHORT CIRCULAR WALKS IN SOUTH YORKSHIRE
SHORT CIRCULAR WALKS IN SOUTH DERBYSHIRE
SHORT CIRCULAR WALKS AROUND BUXTON
SHORT CIRCULAR WALKS AROUND WIRKSWORTH
SHORT CIRCULAR WALKS IN THE HOPE VALLEY
40 SHORT CIRCULAR WALKS IN THE PEAK DISTRICT
CIRCULAR WALKS ON KINDER & BLEAKLOW
SHORT CIRCULAR WALKS IN SOUTH NOTTINGHAMSHIRE
SHORT CIRCULAR WALKS IN CHESHIRE
SHORT CIRCULAR WALKS IN WEST YORKSHIRE
WHITE PEAK DISTRICT AIRCRAFT WRECKS
CIRCULAR WALKS IN THE DERBYSHIRE DALES
SHORT CIRCULAR WALKS FROM BAKEWELL
SHORT CIRCULAR WALKS IN LATHKILL DALE
CIRCULAR WALKS IN THE WHITE PEAK
SHORT CIRCULAR WALKS IN EAST DEVON
SHORT CIRCULAR WALKS AROUND HARROGATE
SHORT CIRCULAR WALKS IN CHARNWOOD FOREST
SHORT CIRCULAR WALKS AROUND CHESTERFIELD
SHORT CIRCULAR WALKS IN THE YORKS DALES - Vol 1 - Southern area.
SHORT CIRCULAR WALKS IN THE AMBER VALLEY (Derbyshire)
SHORT CIRCULAR WALKS IN THE LAKE DISTRICT
SHORT CIRCULAR WALKS IN THE NORTH YORKSHIRE MOORS
SHORT CIRCULAR WALKS IN EAST STAFFORDSHIRE
LONG CIRCULAR WALKS IN THE PEAK DISTRICT - Vol.1, 2 , 3, 4 AND 5.
DARK PEAK AIRCRAFT WRECK WALKS
LONG CIRCULAR WALKS IN THE STAFFORDSHIRE MOORLANDS
LONG CIRCULAR WALKS IN CHESHIRE
WALKING THE TISSINGTON TRAIL
WALKING THE HIGH PEAK TRAIL
WALKING THE MONSAL TRAIL & SETT VALLEY TRAILS
PEAK DISTRICT WALKING - TEN "TEN MILER'S" - Vol One AND Two
CLIMB THE PEAKS OF THE PEAK DISTRICT
PEAK DISTRICT WALK A MONTH Vols One,Two, Three, Four, Five & Six
TRAIN TO WALK Vol. One - The Hope Valley Line
DERBYSHIRE LOST VILLAGE WALKS -Vol One and Two.
CIRCULAR WALKS IN DOVEDALE AND THE MANIFOLD VALLEY
CIRCULAR WALKS AROUND GLOSSOP
WALKING THE LONGDENDALE TRAIL
WALKING THE UPPER DON TRAIL
SHORT CIRCULAR WALKS IN CANNOCK CHASE
CIRCULAR WALKS IN THE DERWENT VALLEY
WALKING THE TRAILS OF NORTH-EAST DERBYSHIRE
WALKING THE PENNINE BRIDLEWAY & CIRCULAR WALKS
SHORT CIRCULAR WALKS ON THE NEW RIVER & SOUTH-EAST HERTFORDSHIRE
SHORT CIRCULAR WALKS IN EPPING FOREST
WALKING THE STREETS OF LONDON
LONG CIRCULAR WALKS IN EASTERN HERTFORDSHIRE
LONG CIRCULAR WALKS IN WESTERN HERTFORDSHIRE
WALKS IN THE LONDON BOROUGH OF ENFIELD

For a free complete catalogue of John Merrill walk Guides send a SAE to The John Merrill Foundation

CANAL WALKS -
VOL 1 - DERBYSHIRE & NOTTINGHAMSHIRE
VOL 2 - CHESHIRE & STAFFORDSHIRE
VOL 3 - STAFFORDSHIRE
VOL 4 - THE CHESHIRE RING
VOL 5 - THE GRANTHAM CANAL
VOL 6 - SOUTH YORKSHIRE
VOL 7 - THE TRENT & MERSEY CANAL
VOL 8 - WALKING THE DERBY CANAL RING
VOL 9 - WALKING THE LLANGOLLEN CANAL
VOL 10 - CIRCULAR WALKS ON THE CHESTERFIELD CANAL
VOL 11 - CIRCULAR WALKS ON THE CROMFORD CANAL
VOL.13 - SHORT CIRCULAR WALKS ON THE RIVER LEE NAVIGATION -Vol. 1 - North
VOL. 14 - SHORT CIRCULAR WALKS ON THE RIVER STORT NAVIGATION
VOL.15 - SHORT CIRCULAR WALKS ON THE RIVER LEE NAVIGATION - Vol. 2 - South
VOL. 16 - WALKING THE CANALS OF LONDON
VOL 17 - WALKING THE RIVER LEE NAVIGATION

Visit our website -
www.johnmerrillwalkguides.com

JOHN MERRILL DAY CHALLENGE WALKS -
WHITE PEAK CHALLENGE WALK
THE HAPPY HIKER - WHITE PEAK - CHALLENGE WALK No.2
DARK PEAK CHALLENGE WALK
PEAK DISTRICT END TO END WALKS
STAFFORDSHIRE MOORLANDS CHALLENGE WALK
THE LITTLE JOHN CHALLENGE WALK
YORKSHIRE DALES CHALLENGE WALK

NORTH YORKSHIRE MOORS CHALLENGE WALK
LAKELAND CHALLENGE WALK
THE RUTLAND WATER CHALLENGE WALK
MALVERN HILLS CHALLENGE WALK
THE SALTER'S WAY
THE SNOWDON CHALLENGE
CHARNWOOD FOREST CHALLENGE WALK
THREE COUNTIES CHALLENGE WALK (PEAK DISTRICT).
CAL-DER-WENT WALK BY GEOFFREY CARR,
THE QUANTOCK WAY
BELVOIR WITCHES CHALLENGE WALK
THE CARNEDDAU CHALLENGE WALK
THE SWEET PEA CHALLENGE WALK
THE LINCOLNSHIRE WOLDS - BLACK DEATH - CHALLENGE WALK
JENNIFER'S CHALLENGE WALK
THE EPPING FOREST CHALLENGE WALK

INSTRUCTION & RECORD -
HIKE TO BE FIT.....STROLLING WITH JOHN
THE JOHN MERRILL WALK RECORD BOOK
HIKE THE WORLD - JOHN MERRILL'S GUIDE TO WALKING & BACKPACKING.

MULTIPLE DAY WALKS -
THE RIVERS'S WAY
PEAK DISTRICT: HIGH LEVEL ROUTE
PEAK DISTRICT MARATHONS
THE LIMEY WAY
THE PEAKLAND WAY
COMPO'S WAY BY ALAN HILEY
THE BRIGHTON WAY BY NORMAN WILLIS

THE PILGRIM WALKS SERIES -
THE WALSINGHAM WAY - ELY TO WALSINGHAM - 72 MILES
THE WALSINGHAM WAY - KINGS LYNN TO WALSINGHAM - 35 MILES
TURN LEFT AT GRANJA DE LA MORERUELA - 700 MILES
NORTH TO SANTIAGO DE COMPOSTELA, VIA FATIMA - 650 MILES
ST. OLAV'S WAY - OSLO TO TRONDHEIM - 400 MILES
ST. WINEFRIDE'S WAY - ST. ASAPH TO HOLYWELL
ST. ALBANS WAY - WALTHAM ABBEY TO ST. ALBANS - 26 MILES
ST. KENELM TRAIL BY JOHN PRICE - CLENT HILLS TO WINCHCOMBE - 60 MILES
DERBYSHIRE PILGRIMAGES

COAST WALKS & NATIONAL TRAILS -
ISLE OF WIGHT COAST PATH
PEMBROKESHIRE COAST PATH
THE CLEVELAND WAY
WALKING ANGELSEY'S COASTLINE.
WALKING THE COASTLINE OF THE CHANNEL ISLANDS

DERBYSHIRE & PEAK DISTRICT HISTORICAL GUIDES -
A TO Z GUIDE OF THE PEAK DISTRICT
DERBYSHIRE INNS - AN A TO Z GUIDE
HALLS AND CASTLES OF THE PEAK DISTRICT & DERBYSHIRE
TOURING THE PEAK DISTRICT & DERBYSHIRE BY CAR
DERBYSHIRE FOLKLORE
PUNISHMENT IN DERBYSHIRE
CUSTOMS OF THE PEAK DISTRICT & DERBYSHIRE
WINSTER - A SOUVENIR GUIDE
ARKWRIGHT OF CROMFORD
LEGENDS OF DERBYSHIRE
DERBYSHIRE FACTS & RECORDS
TALES FROM THE MINES BY GEOFFREY CARR
PEAK DISTRICT PLACE NAMES BY MARTIN SPRAY
DERBYSHIRE THROUGH THE AGES - VOL 1 -DERBYSHIRE IN PREHISTORIC TIMES
SIR JOSEPH PAXTON
FLORENCE NIGHTINGALE
JOHN SMEDLEY
BONNIE PRINCE CHARLIE & 20 MILE WALK.
THE STORY OF THE EARLS AND DUKES OF DEVONSHIRE

For a free complete catalogue of John Merrill walk Guides send a SAE to The John Merrill Foundation

JOHN MERRILL'S MAJOR WALKS -
TURN RIGHT AT LAND'S END
WITH MUSTARD ON MY BACK
TURN RIGHT AT DEATH VALLEY
EMERALD COAST WALK
I CHOSE TO WALK - WHY I WALK ETC.
A WALK IN OHIO - 1,310 MILES AROUND THE BUCKEYE TRAIL.

Visit our website -
www.johnmerrillwalkguides.com

SKETCH BOOKS -
SKETCHES OF THE PEAK DISTRICT

COLOUR BOOK:-
THE PEAK DISTRICT.......SOMETHING TO REMEMBER HER BY.

OVERSEAS GUIDES -
HIKING IN NEW MEXICO - VOL I - THE SANDIA AND MANZANO MOUNTAINS.
VOL 2 - HIKING "BILLY THE KID" COUNTRY. VOL 4 - N.W. AREA - " HIKING INDIAN COUNTRY."
"WALKING IN DRACULA COUNTRY" - ROMANIA.
WALKING THE TRAILS OF THE HONG KONG ISLANDS.

VISITOR GUIDES - MATLOCK . BAKEWELL. ASHBOURNE.

Staffordshire Books -

from JOHN N. MERRILL
EMAIL - marathonhikeraol.com

125 SHORT CIRCULAR WALKS IN EAST STAFFORDSHIRE - £6.95

106 SHORT CIRCULAR WALKS IN THE STAFFS MOORS - £6.95

201 LONG CIRCULAR WALKS IN THE STAFFS MOORS - £7.95

404 STAFFS MOORLANDS CHALLENGE WALK - £3.95

302 CHESHIRE & STAFFORDSHIRE CANAL WALKS - £8.95

303 STAFFORDSHIRE CANAL WALKS -£8.95

307 THE TRENT AND MERSEY CANAL - £6.95

363 CYCLING AROUND STAFFORDSHIRE - £7.95

153 CIRCULAR WALKS IN CANNOCK CHASE - £6.95